THE CHEF
AND THE
SLOW COOKER

HUGH ACHESON

PHOTOGRAPHS BY ANDREW THOMAS LEE

CLARKSON POTTER/PUBLISHERS
NEW YORK

Library of Congress Cataloging-in-Publication Data

Names: Acheson, Hugh, author.

Title: The chef and the slow cooker / Hugh Acheson; photographs by Andrew Thomas Lee.

Description: First edition. | New York : Clarkson Potter/Publishers, 2017 |

Identifiers: LCCN 2017005293 (print) | LCCN 2017011173 (ebook) |

ISBN 9780451498540 (hardcover) | ISBN 9780451498557 (ebook)

Subjects: LCSH: Electric cooking, Slow. | LCGFT: Cookbooks.

Classification: LCC TX827 (ebook) | LCC TX827 .A24 2017 (print) | DDC 641.5/884—dc23

LC record available at https://lccn.loc.gov/2017005293.

ISBN 978-0-451-49854-0

Ebook ISBN 978-0-451-49855-7

Printed in the United States of America

Illustrations by Hugh Acheson

Design by Stephanie Huntwork

Jacket photographs by Andrew Thomas Lee

10 9 8 7 6 5 4 3 2

First Edition

CONTENTS

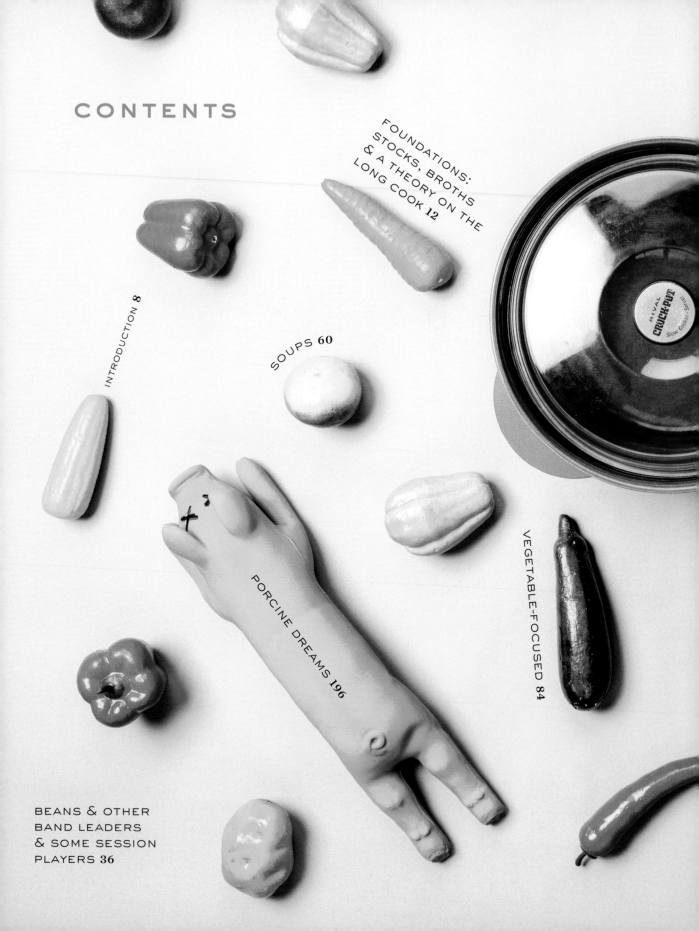

INTRODUCTION

You have a slow cooker. Somewhere. Your mother gave it to you when you went away to school. Or you got one for a wedding present from that strange aunt who wears a bright green muumuu every day of her life. Or you got one from your bank for opening a savings account. Maybe it's in the back of the closet with that cold-press juicer that you used twice, or in the garage under the boxes of old tax returns that you probably could shred by now.

You should find it, or if you really can't find it because it wisped away in the last move or at that potluck you went to down the street four years ago, then go buy one. Because I want you to speak in its particular language of cooking. I want to show you how to use that slow cooker. Slow cookers are an old-school technology that will guide you to better meals in this contemporary world.

Slow cooking goes way beyond the ubiquitous pot roast (though there certainly is nothing wrong with a great pot roast). What a slow cooker does is actually really important in our modern world: It gives you time. Time to walk away from the kitchen—sometimes for an hour, and sometimes for eight. What you do with that time is up to you, but I suggest doing those things that mean a lot to you. Do things that you yearn to do more of: read a book that you keep putting down, walk with no destination in mind, write that limerick about your boss that you have been itching to get done, change that lightbulb that has been out for a year, organize the spice drawer, learn how to crochet . . . the possibilities are endless. I want you to have time to be a better you.

So why is slow cooking on our minds these days? 'Cause we need to be cooking from scratch again, applying ourselves in the kitchen. But given

Breville

the lives we live, it can be hard to find the time to devote to the thing that should be paramount in our lives: nourishment, the act of feeding yourself and the ones you love. We need nourishment in our lives, now more than ever. We do not create cherished memories of family and food over pizza pockets. And getting well acquainted with your slow cooker is a great way of nourishing yourself and your family while saving you the time that those pizza pockets promise.

The beauty of the cooker is that it's a shortcut that doesn't sacrifice quality or taste. You may be wondering, why not just use a regular large braising pot? Ahh . . . where to start: that beautiful pot weighs more than a V-8 engine and is next to impossible to clean in a regular-size sink. Finding that simmering point on your stove, ensuring a consistent temperature, is like figuring out Fermat's last theorem, and, well, that probably ain't gonna happen. The slow cooker has a thermostat making that simmer the same every time. The slow cooker doesn't have to be over the open flame, and thus it doesn't have to be monitored like something that wants to burn your house down. The slow cooker is a device that makes life more productive and enjoyable by freeing you up to do other things.

Let us chat about the technology of the cooker itself. Most are very simple: there is a low setting for low heat and a high setting for a high heat—those being different ends of the spectrum of what we call "simmering" in the language of cooking. Newer versions have a dial to control temperature, timers, automatic shut-offs, steam settings, searing ability, and rice-cooking functions, but really those bells and whistles are ancillary to the core idea of what this book is about. I am about the old school: the low simmer and the high simmer.

The real key is to find a model with a heavy porcelain or weighty enameled insert, like choosing a heavy pot versus a crappy aluminum one, because heat dispersion is important when we think about slow cooking. You want the heat to be evenly distributed, with few "hot spots." Some slow

LOW
OFF   HIGH

RIVAL
CROCK·POT

FOUNDATIONS:
STOCKS, BROTHS
& a theory on the long cook

Stocks and broths are essential building blocks in cooking, and a homemade stock or broth elevates a dish above the rest. These workhorses provide the basis of flavor to dishes, create nuance, and give backbone to long-simmered meats and vegetables. Long cooking should be like a Jacuzzi for the main ingredient—a gentle hot tub of delightful flavors that are gradually extracted and become unified—and the consistent temperature of a slow cooker makes it the perfect vehicle.

All of the recipes in this chapter, with the exception of the dashi and the consommé, are pretty mindless, walk-away-from-the-pot types, and are perfect for a workday.

One thing to keep in mind: When you are cooking ingredients for a long time, their flavors tend to meld, deepen, and in some cases become dull and taste overcooked. (Think of the army-green peas in your school cafeteria.) That's why stocks, and other dishes that require a long cooking time, will generally call for you to cut the flavor-imparting vegetables into large pieces. If you finely dice carrots and put them in a chicken stock that is going to cook for eight hours, you will have a flavor akin to overcooked carrots; but if you cut the carrots in large pieces to release their flavor more slowly, then you will have something delicious. So think about that when looking at your ingredients. You can also add more vegetables later on during the cook time to keep that fresh, bright flavor.

I try to make a batch of some type of stock each week. It is a rewarding exercise that makes the house smell great. Stocks and broths keep well in the fridge for about a week, and they also freeze well. I freeze mine in wide-mouth glass jars with about an inch of air space to account for expansion. You can freeze them in sealable plastic bags as well, which is sometimes the best option in a packed freezer. Ice cube trays work too, and are great because they allow you to add that little bit of stock a dish might need. Once the stock is frozen in the ice cube trays, remove the cubes from the tray and transfer them to a sealable plastic bag. Unless you lose power in a storm or your freezer dies, frozen stocks and broths will keep for up to six months.

Slow Cooker
Chicken Broth

SLOW COOKER SIZE: **6+ QUARTS**
MAKES **4 QUARTS**
PREP TIME: **15 MINUTES**
COOK TIME: **8 TO 12 HOURS**

We use a lot of slow cooker chicken broth in my house. It is a beautiful thing when crafted from scratch, and who knew it could be so easy? Drop all of the ingredients in and walk away. It's like a culinary mic drop. This recipe is technically a broth, not a stock, because it's made from meat as well as bones, giving it richer flavor, but you can certainly use stock wherever you'd use this broth, and vice versa.

1 whole chicken (3 to 4 pounds), head removed, but feet are good if they are attached

½ teaspoon kosher salt

2 garlic cloves

Several sprigs fresh thyme

Several sprigs fresh flat-leaf parsley

2 bay leaves

2 medium white onions, quartered

3 large carrots, cut into 2-inch lengths

3 celery stalks with leaves, cut into 2-inch lengths

1 teaspoon coriander seeds

6 black peppercorns

1   Butcher the chicken (see page 133). Keep the gizzards, heart, neck, and backbone for the broth, but set the liver aside for another day. (Livers are great to accumulate in the freezer for use in a pâté or to finish a sauce.) Season the chicken pieces with the salt.

2   Put the chicken pieces in a slow cooker, and add the garlic, thyme and parsley sprigs, bay leaves, onions, carrots, celery, coriander, and peppercorns. Add 4 quarts of cold water, or enough to cover. Cover with the lid, turn the cooker to the low setting, and walk away for 8 to 12 hours (some people call that going to work, but you could do whatever you want).

3   Strain the broth into containers, discarding the solids, and use it within 5 days or freeze it for up to 6 months.

Dark Chicken Broth

French cuisine is based on some formidable broths and stocks that definitely don't come in boxes. They provide depth and oomph to food. They resonate. They smell wonderful. And this is one of them. It's not quite as simple as dropping the ingredients in and walking away, but the extra step of deeply browning the chicken adds an incredible layer of flavor that is the backbone of many great dishes.

1 whole chicken (3 to 4 pounds), head removed, but feet are good if they are attached

1 teaspoon olive oil

½ teaspoon kosher salt

2 garlic cloves

3 tablespoons tomato paste

Several sprigs fresh thyme

Several sprigs fresh flat-leaf parsley

2 bay leaves

2 medium white onions, quartered

3 large carrots, cut into 2-inch lengths

3 celery stalks with leaves, cut into 2-inch lengths

1 teaspoon coriander seeds

6 black peppercorns

1 Butcher the chicken (see page 133). Set the breast and liver aside for other uses, keeping the thighs, wings, drumsticks, backbone, breastbone, gizzards, heart, and neck for this broth.

2 Place the largest skillet you have over medium-low heat and add the olive oil to the pan. Season the thighs, wings, and drumsticks with the salt. Then place them, skin-side down, in the skillet and crisp them slowly until they are deeply browned, about 30 minutes. Turn the chicken pieces over and cook for 10 minutes more. Remove the chicken from the skillet and place all of the pieces—including the backbone, breastbone, gizzards, heart, and neck—into a slow cooker.

3 Discard the rendered fat in the skillet and place the skillet over medium heat. Add 1 cup of water and scrape up the good browned bits that are stuck to the bottom of the pan. Pour these pan drippings into the slow cooker. Add the garlic, tomato paste, thyme and parsley sprigs, bay leaves, onions, carrots, celery, coriander, and peppercorns. Add 4 quarts of cold water, or enough to cover. Cover with the lid, turn the cooker to the low setting, and cook for 8 hours.

4 Strain the broth into containers, discarding the solids, and use it within 5 days or freeze it for up to 6 months.

Fish Stock

Most fish stocks, called *fumets* in French, are made on the stove in under an hour. But using a slow cooker lets you extract all the flavor out of the bones in a gentle way. Salmon bones are okay. White fish bones are better. Halibut are best. The darker and oily fish do not make good stocks—they exude too much fishiness. Lean white fish like flounder and halibut work best for clean, clear stocks. Fish stock adds versatility to your pantry. With the finished stock you can make a panoply of dishes, like fish soups, stews, sauces, and braises. Or just sauté some aromatics, add them to the fish stock, simmer some vegetables in it, and then drop in any seasoned seafood to gently poach until just cooked. You'll have a wonderful meal.

3 pounds fish bones, soaked in water overnight and drained to purge the blood

1 cup dry white wine

2 medium leeks (white and light green parts), halved lengthwise and rinsed well, then cut into 1-inch lengths

4 celery stalks, large-diced

1 medium fennel bulb, large-diced

4 bay leaves

1 cup minced fresh flat-leaf parsley stems

1 tablespoon coriander seeds

1 teaspoon fennel seeds

8 black peppercorns

1 teaspoon kosher salt

1   Put the drained fish bones and the white wine in a slow cooker. Then add the leeks, celery, fennel, bay leaves, parsley, coriander and fennel seeds, peppercorns, and salt. Pour in 4 quarts of cold water, cover with the lid, turn the cooker to the low setting, and cook for 4 hours.

2   Skim any foam off the top and strain the stock into containers, discarding the solids. Use the stock within 5 days or freeze it for up to 6 months.

FISH STOCK

Shrimp Stock

SLOW COOKER SIZE: **6+ QUARTS**
MAKES **4 QUARTS**
PREP TIME: **20 MINUTES**
COOK TIME: **4 HOURS**

Use this stock to poach fish, make risotto, cook the grits for your shrimp and grits, or as a base for gumbo or bouillabaisse. It is a simple recipe that supplies a ton of flavor on its own, but if you want to add an accent, think lemon, lemongrass, or lime leaf. It really is a great use of shrimp shells, and it also freezes well. I freeze shrimp shells whenever I am peeling shrimp and when I have enough for a quiet Sunday prep session, I thaw them out and make this stock. This is great to have already made if you embark on the Southern Shrimp Pilau (page 107).

2 tablespoons canola oil

4 cups shrimp shells, patted dry

1 large yellow onion, minced

2 stalks celery, minced

3 garlic cloves, crushed

1 (1-inch) piece fresh ginger, thinly sliced

2 tablespoons tomato paste

1 cup dry sake or white wine

1 sprig fresh thyme

Handful of flat-leaf parsley stems, cut into 1-inch lengths

1 tablespoon coriander seeds, toasted

4 bay leaves

Pinch of crushed red pepper flakes

1   Preheat a slow cooker on the low setting for at least 20 minutes.

2   In a large frying pan or wok, heat the oil over high heat until it is nearly smoking. Add the shrimp shells and cook, stirring often, until they are bright pink and very aromatic, 3 minutes. (You can also do this in the slow cooker itself, set on high, but you will need to cook it for a longer time to really dry out and toast the shells.) Add the onion, celery, garlic, and ginger and cook until the vegetables have softened, 3 minutes. Add the tomato paste, stir well to incorporate it, and remove the pan from the heat. Deglaze the pan with the sake and add the thyme, parsley stems, coriander seeds, bay leaves, and red pepper flakes. Pour the contents of the pan into the preheated slow cooker and add 4 quarts of cold water. Cover with the lid and cook on the low setting for 4 hours.

3   Strain the stock into containers, discarding the solids. Store it in the refrigerator for up to 5 days, or freeze it for up to 6 months.

Veg Stock

Vegetable Stock

SLOW COOKER SIZE: **6+ QUARTS**
MAKES **4 QUARTS**
PREP TIME: **10 MINUTES**
COOK TIME: **3 HOURS**

I've always loved vegetables, but I was anti–vegetable stock for a long time. I fought a noble fight against dank, watery eau-de-overcooked-vegetables. But I am getting older, more mature in my ways, and more accepting of things. I can now see the other side: with the growing number of vegetarians who visit my tables, I have found that a really good vegetable stock gives me an option to make soups, vegetable stews, sauces, and pasta dishes that will make everyone happy. And so I created a vegetable stock that even I can love. Just don't go mauling it with vegetables that are beyond their prime. Make it with love and respect and it'll love and respect you back.

3 large yellow onions, large-diced

3 large carrots, large-diced

3 stalks celery, large-diced

2 garlic cloves, cut in half

1 lemon, cut in half

4 bay leaves

2 sprigs fresh thyme

1 tablespoon black peppercorns

1 tablespoon coriander seeds

1 Combine the onions, carrots, celery, and garlic in a slow cooker. Add the lemon halves, bay leaves, thyme sprigs, peppercorns, and coriander seeds. Pour in 4 quarts of cold water, cover with the lid, set the slow cooker to the high setting, and cook for 3 hours.

2 Strain the stock into containers, discarding the vegetables. Use the stock within 1 week or freeze it for up to 6 months.

Dashi

Dashi, with its clean but complex umami-rich quality, is the versatile mother stock of Japan, and it should be in your repertoire. The best way to expand our culinary horizons is to understand the foundational bricks of other cuisines. So many Japanese dishes use dashi that you'll put it to work quickly: miso soup, ponzu sauce, simple braises, and a multitude of stews. It is a workhorse. But don't feel that you need to use it only in Japanese dishes—its flavor is deep but so light and versatile that you can use it in lots of dishes that call for chicken or even vegetable stock. Dashi is a simply made stock—about the quickest stock there is—and it freezes well, so don't worry about having too much. You can find the ingredients in specialty markets, in Asian groceries, or online.

3 ounces kombu (a dried seaweed)

½ ounce dried bonito flakes (dried tuna, called *katsuobushi*)

1   Combine 4 quarts of cold water and the kombu in a 4-quart or larger slow cooker and turn it to the high setting. Cover with the lid and cook for 1 hour.

2   Remove the kombu with tongs, discard, and add the bonito flakes to the liquid. Turn off the slow cooker and steep the bonito flakes for 5 minutes. Then strain the dashi into containers and discard the solids. Use it within 5 days or freeze it for up to 4 months.

Pho Broth

SLOW COOKER SIZE: **6+ QUARTS**
MAKES ABOUT **3 QUARTS**
PREP TIME: **30 MINUTES**
COOK TIME: **8 TO 10 HOURS**

Yeah, this broth has a lot of meat matter in it, but what results is a clean and amazing base to one of the most nourishing soups in the world. Pho is the classic Vietnamese bowl of rice noodles, clear beef broth with sweet spices, and slices of both braised and just-poached beef on top. You make people happy with pho. So go on, make people happy. In this recipe, the chuck is pulled out after a period and reserved for making pho, and the rest of the beef bones are strained away after prolonged cooking. If you want to make the broth but not prepare pho, that's fine. You will have made a bone broth with tons of flavor. Consume it in place of tea or coffee and feel like a healthier human.

1 tablespoon canola oil

3 medium yellow onions, unpeeled, cut in half

½ pound fresh ginger, unpeeled, cut into 4 large pieces

1 head garlic, unpeeled

1 pound oxtails

2 pounds beef shin bones, cut into 2-inch lengths by the butcher

2 pounds beef chuck, left whole

1 (3-inch) piece of cinnamon stick

½ tablespoon whole cloves

1 tablespoon fennel seeds

1 tablespoon coriander seeds

4 star anise pods

¼ cup fish sauce

1½ tablespoons sugar

1 Preheat the oven to 400°F, and preheat a slow cooker on the high setting for at least 15 minutes.

2 While the slow cooker heats up, set a large cast-iron skillet over medium-high heat. Add the canola oil and place the onions, cut-side down, in the pan. Add the ginger and the whole head of garlic, transfer the skillet to the oven, and roast the onions, ginger, and garlic for 30 minutes, until everything is well charred.

3 Meanwhile, put the oxtails, shin bones, and chuck into a large pot and add water to cover by 1 inch. Place the pot over high heat and bring the liquid to a boil. Boil for 15 minutes, frequently skimming off any foam that rises to the surface. Skim once more and then carefully drain the bones and meat in a large colander, discarding the liquid. Transfer the drained meats to the slow cooker and add the charred vegetables along with the cinnamon stick, cloves, fennel seeds, coriander seeds, and star anise. Pour in 4 quarts of lukewarm water. Add the fish sauce and the sugar. Cover with the lid and cook on the high setting for 2 hours.

4 Uncover the slow cooker and skim off the fat that has risen to the surface. Remove the chuck, place it on a plate, and put it in the refrigerator to chill (reserve it for making Pho with Chuck and Rib Eye, page 33). Re-cover the slow cooker and cook the broth on the high setting for 6 to 8 more hours.

5 Strain the broth, discarding all the solids, and drink it now as the delicious bone broth that it is, or use it within a couple of days for pho. Otherwise, freeze it for up to 6 months.

Beef Consommé

Consommé is an old-school soup, but one that is beloved by chefs because it's so clean and flavorful. Consommé is the result of a technique called "fining"—essentially a process of clarifying in which you slowly cook a mixture of stock, vegetables, ground meat, and egg whites. While it cooks, the egg whites float to the surface, lifting the vegetables and meat to the top and filtering the broth as they do so. This results in a "raft" of vegetables and meat, held together with the cooked egg whites, and a crystal-clear broth underneath. On the stove, this is a tricky technique because you have to keep the temperature consistent. In a slow cooker, you can walk away.

Consommés can be served hot or cold, and sometimes even fully gelled when chilled. They can be lovely, brothy sauces for delicate dishes, like a poached beef loin with winter vegetables. And if you are under the weather, there is no better corpse-reviver than a cup of hot consommé with a squeeze of lemon in it. If you need more than that, call the doctor.

Note: You will need a conical sieve and some cheesecloth to strain the consommé properly. In a pinch coffee filters and a colander work too.

3 quarts Beef Shin Stock (page 21)

2 pounds lean ground beef

1 large carrot, diced

2 medium leeks (white and light green parts), rinsed well and diced

1 cup diced butternut squash

1 medium tomato, diced, or 1 cup canned tomatoes

6 egg whites

2 tablespoons fresh thyme leaves

2 tablespoons chopped flat-leaf parsley leaves

1 teaspoon coriander seeds

4 bay leaves

8 black peppercorns

Kosher salt

1   Pour the stock into a slow cooker and turn it to the high setting. Cover with the lid and cook until the stock is warmed through, at least 30 minutes.

2   Meanwhile, place the ground beef in a large bowl. Combine the carrot, leeks, squash, and tomato in a food processor and pulse until the mixture reaches a fine mince. In a separate bowl, whisk the egg whites until they are smooth and lightly aerated; then add the whites to the mixture in the food processor and pulse just to incorporate. Add this mixture, along with the thyme, parsley, coriander, bay leaves, and peppercorns, to the ground beef. Mix well, then add the whole mixture to the warmed stock in the slow cooker. Mix well with a spoon or a

whisk. Cover with the lid and cook on the high setting for 30 minutes.

3   Stir the stock gently with the whisk or spoon to make sure that nothing is adhering to the bottom of the cooker. Then re-cover the cooker and cook until a firm raft forms on top of the liquid, 1½ to 2 hours.

4   Take a small ladle and gently break a hole about 4 inches wide in the middle of the raft. Ladle any loose matter back over the solid part of the raft to remove it from the clarified stock. Turn off the heat.

5   Place a conical sieve lined with cheesecloth over a large, clean container. Carefully ladle the clear broth from the hole you created, pouring it into the sieve to strain away any small pieces of vegetable. When all the consommé is in the container, discard the raft and the strained solids. Season the consommé with salt to taste.

6   Serve the consommé within the next 5 days, or freeze it for up to 6 months.

BEANS

& other band leaders & some session players

Beans and their leguminous brethren are strong building blocks for many meals, and the recipes herein are used in that way, though many do taste great on their own. We should all be eating more beans: they're inexpensive, great for you, a good source of protein, and if they satisfy you enough so that you eat a little less meat, they'll be great for the environment, too. Most any bean you find in your market is tasty, but I want you to find beans that matter. Rancho Gordo is a California broker of some of the best organically grown oddball beans, with great quality, flavor, and texture. Anson Mills is a South Carolina–based grain specialist for heritage corn, beans, and grains of the highest order. Both have websites where you can order their products. Or look into your neighborhood places, particularly at grocery stores that serve a bean-loving clientele, such as the Hispanic *supermercado*, the Indian grocery, or the Korean market.

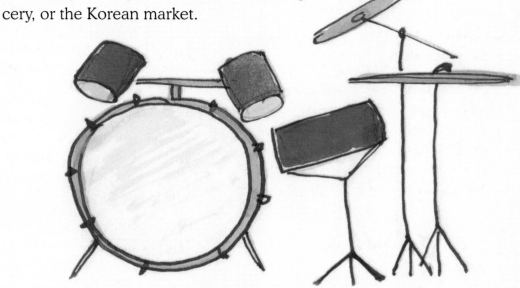

Refried Beans with Duck Fat, Cotija & Red Onion

SLOW COOKER SIZE: **4+ QUARTS**
SERVES **6 TO 8 AS A SIDE**
PREP TIME: **15 TO 20 MINUTES**
COOK TIME: **2 TO 3 HOURS PLUS 20 MINUTES FINISHING PREP**

These beans are a great staple to add to your repertoire. They are so easy and tasty, you'll never want canned refried beans again. Typically, refried beans are made with lard, but the duck fat is a fun twist that adds a depth of flavor that is hard to describe. It's easy to find duck fat online, in fancier grocery stores, or at the butcher.

1 pound dried pinto beans

6 garlic cloves

4 bay leaves

2 sprigs fresh oregano

Kosher salt

½ cup duck fat

1 medium red onion, minced

2 cups Slow Cooker Chicken Broth (page 17)

¼ cup crumbled Cotija cheese

2 tablespoons finely chopped fresh cilantro leaves and stems

¼ cup sliced Pickled Jalapeños (recipe follows)

1   Place the beans in a large saucepan and add cold water to cover by 3 inches. Add the garlic, bay leaves, and oregano sprigs. Bring to a boil and then boil the beans for 5 minutes. Pour the contents of the pot into a slow cooker, cover with the lid, turn the cooker to the high setting, and cook until tender, 2 to 3 hours. Drain the beans and place them in a large heatproof bowl (discard the garlic, bay leaves, and oregano sprigs). Add 2 teaspoons salt and stir well to incorporate.

2   Place a large skillet over medium-high heat and add the duck fat. When the fat is hot but not smoking, add the onion and cook until translucent, 3 minutes. Add the beans and cook for 5 minutes, stirring every once in a while. Season with salt, if desired. (You may need to do this in batches, depending on the size of your skillet; just be sure to reserve a portion of the onion to cook with each batch.)

3   Transfer half of the beans to a blender or food processor, add the chicken broth, and puree until smooth. Return the pureed beans to the skillet and stir to incorporate and rewarm.

4   Platter up the beans however you'd like and garnish them with the Cotija cheese, cilantro, and Pickled Jalapeño slices.

PICKLED JALAPEÑOS

MAKES 1 QUART

1 pound fresh jalapeños, scored with a small X at the bottom end

¼ cup thinly sliced carrot

¼ red onion, sliced

2 bay leaves

3 garlic cloves, smashed

1 teaspoon dried Mexican oregano

1 tablespoon fresh thyme leaves

1 tablespoon kosher salt

1 teaspoon sugar

2 cups cider vinegar

1   Combine all the ingredients in a nonreactive pot and bring to a boil. Reduce the heat to maintain a simmer and cook for 10 minutes.

2   Using a wide-mouth canning funnel, pour the contents into a clean quart (or two 1-pint) jars, leaving ½ inch of headspace. Cap with the lid and band, allow to cool for 2 hours, and then either refrigerate or process according to the jar manufacturer's directions.

3   The jalapeños can be refrigerated for 7 to 10 days; if processed, they will keep for up to 10 months.

Oatmeal with Maple Syrup, Pear, Pecans & Pecan Milk

SLOW COOKER SIZE: **4 QUARTS**
SERVES **4**
PREP TIME: **5 MINUTES**
COOK TIME: **4 TO 8 HOURS**

The idea of making oatmeal in a slow cooker may be strange, but it makes breakfast the easiest meal ever. (Okay, instant oatmeal exists, but it's actually made from ground-up newspapers. I haven't proven that yet, but it tastes like it.) Use steel-cut oats, which have wonderful flavor but need actual cooking. With this recipe, the oats cook while you sleep, but max it out at 8 hours—the magic amount of sleep required to be a responsible, healthy, and productive human. You can easily increase or decrease the quantities in this recipe according to the number of folks you will be feeding.

Nut milks are everywhere these days, but the best comes from our friends at Treehouse Milk. They make organic, pure, and wonderful pecan milk. And it is local to us. And they are our friends. So, find some friends who make nut milk and support them. Or, you could prepare this with regular milk if you want. I am not watching you, but nut milks are a glorious thing to start incorporating into your cooking.

1 cup steel-cut oats

2 pears, cored and diced

½ cup chopped toasted pecans

¼ cup maple syrup

1 teaspoon kosher salt

1 cup pecan milk, or other milk of your choosing

1   Combine the oats, pears, pecans, half of the maple syrup, and the salt in a slow cooker, and turn the cooker to the low setting. Add 4 cups of cold water, cover with the lid, and cook for 4 to 8 hours, depending on how much you sleep. I don't sleep much.

2   Season the cooked oatmeal with additional salt, if desired. To serve, divide the oatmeal among 4 bowls. Using a spoon, make a well in the center of each portion and pour in the pecan milk. Drizzle with the remaining maple syrup, 'cause maple syrup rules.

White Bean Soup with Ham Hock & Escarole

SLOW COOKER SIZE: **4+ QUARTS**
SERVES **4 TO 6**
PREP TIME: **OVERNIGHT SOAK PLUS 10 MINUTES**
COOK TIME: **6 TO 8 HOURS**

White beans and ham hock are a match made in heaven. When finished with the bitter beauty of escarole, this soup becomes a meal. And it is even better reheated the next day for a quick lunch.

½ pound dried white beans, such as cannellini

1 smoked ham hock (about 1 pound)

2 tablespoons unsalted butter

1 small sweet onion, minced

1 celery stalk, minced

2 carrots, minced

A couple sprigs each of fresh thyme, rosemary, bay leaf, and parsley, tied together

¼-pound piece of Parmigiano-Reggiano rind

4 cups finely chopped escarole (about 1 head)

Pinch of crushed red pepper flakes

Kosher salt

1   Place the beans in a large bowl and add cold water to cover by 3 inches. Cover the bowl and soak the beans in the refrigerator for 8 hours or overnight.

2   Drain the beans and place them in a slow cooker. Add 7 cups of fresh water and the ham hock.

3   Place a medium skillet over medium-high heat. Add the butter, and when it bubbles and froths, add the onion. Cook until translucent, 2 minutes. Then add the celery and carrots and cook until softened, 5 minutes. Empty the contents of the skillet directly into the slow cooker. (Alternatively, you can cook the vegetables directly in the slow cooker set on high, but you will likely need to add time to each step.) Add the bundle of herbs and the Parmigiano-Reggiano rind. Cover with the lid, turn the cooker to the low setting, and cook for 6 to 8 hours, until the beans are tender and cooked through.

4   Remove and reserve the ham hock. Discard the cheese rind and the bundle of herbs.

5   When the ham hock is cool enough to handle, pull the meat from the bone; discard the sinew, excess fat, skin, and bone. Chop the meat and return it to the slow cooker. Turn off the heat, stir in the escarole and the red pepper flakes, then season with salt to taste.

6   Ladle the soup into individual bowls and serve.

Grits

Grits are a Southern staple. There are two types: yellow and white hominy. Yellow hominy has a kinship to polenta, and white hominy is made from nixtamalized corn, meaning the dry kernels have been soaked in an alkaline solution. Look for stone-ground grits from a smaller, local mill, because real small-operation gristmills are one aspect of foodways that we should be cherishing and supporting, and fresh-ground grits have a special flavor. Alternatively, you can order stellar grits online from ansonmills.com.

This is a great recipe for a slow cooker because the consistent low heat is ideal for the long cook that grits like. When you're cooking them on the stovetop, it can be difficult to get the exact simmer the grits need, and you can end up with a burnt spot on the bottom of the pot—a small error that can ruin the whole batch. If you want to make the grits with chicken or shrimp stock, by all means do it. This is just a technique, and once you master it you can slow-cook grits with flavorful liquids, with half stock and half milk, or with the addition of Parmesan or crème fraîche at the end.

And yes, you can eat grits for dinner. I do all the time.

2 cups coarsely ground white hominy grits

¼ cup (½ stick) unsalted butter, plus more for serving

Kosher salt and freshly ground black pepper

1   Turn a slow cooker to the low setting. Add 7 cups of cold water to the slow cooker; then pour in the grits, whisking to combine. Add the butter, cover with the lid, and cook for 2 hours.

2   Uncover the cooker, stir the grits well, replace the cover, and cook, stirring every once in a while, for another 2 hours.

3   Season with salt and pepper to taste, and serve with additional pats of butter for melting into the grits.

Cowboy Beans

SLOW COOKER SIZE: **4+ QUARTS**
SERVES **8 AS A SIDE**
PREP TIME: **OVERNIGHT SOAK**
COOK TIME: **6 TO 8 HOURS PLUS 45 MINUTES FOR FINISHING**

Charro beans make for a soupy, meaty, one-pot meal that is a magnet for whatever odds and ends you have on hand. In this case, we use the slow cooker to get the beans nice and creamy, and then finish them with a quick sauté of bacon, pork, chiles, and beer to add a few layers of flavor.

1 pound dried pinto beans

Kosher salt

1 tablespoon canola oil

½ pound slab bacon, minced

½ pound boneless pork shoulder, cut into ½-inch cubes

1 onion, minced

4 garlic cloves, minced

2 poblano chiles, seeded and minced

1 teaspoon cumin seeds, toasted and ground

2 tomatoes, seeded and diced

1 (12-ounce) bottle dark lager beer

Juice of 2 limes

1 cup minced fresh cilantro leaves and stems

1 Place the beans in a large bowl and add cold water to cover by 3 inches. Cover the bowl and soak the beans in the refrigerator for 8 hours or overnight.

2 Drain the beans, place them in a slow cooker, and add fresh water to cover by 2 inches. Cover with the lid, turn the slow cooker to the low setting, and cook until tender, for 6 to 8 hours. Season with salt to taste.

3 When the beans are nearly cooked to your liking, place a large skillet over medium-high heat and warm the oil in it. When the oil begins to shimmer, add the bacon and the cubed pork shoulder and season with salt. Cook until the fat begins to render, about 2 minutes, and then add the onion, garlic, and chiles. Cook for 5 minutes. Then add the cumin, tomatoes, and beer and season with salt again. Stir well, and add the mixture to the beans. Cover and cook on the low setting for 30 minutes; then stir in the lime juice. Serve hot, garnished with the cilantro.

52   THE CHEF & THE SLOW COOKER

Boston "Baked" Beans

SLOW COOKER SIZE: **4+ QUARTS**
SERVES **8 TO 12 AS A SIDE**
PREP TIME: **OVERNIGHT SOAK PLUS 20 MINUTES**
COOK TIME: **6 TO 8 HOURS**

I gotta be honest: I never liked baked beans growing up. They were always too sweet, and I had an aversion to sugar in savory foods. I just couldn't wrap my head around the idea. Things change and palates morph, and I now love me some baked beans, but I still like to have control over the sweetness. This recipe shows restraint, with the sweetness of the molasses balanced by savory mustard and zippy orange zest. I love these baked beans for a simple lunch, or as part of a braised pork dinner.

1 pound dried white beans, such as navy beans

1½ quarts Slow Cooker Chicken Broth (page 17)

1 tablespoon olive oil

½ pound thick-cut bacon, small-diced

1 medium yellow onion, minced (1 cup)

2 garlic cloves, minced

1 teaspoon dry mustard

1 cup blackstrap molasses

1 teaspoon minced orange zest

1 teaspoon chopped fresh thyme leaves

Kosher salt

1 Place the beans in large bowl and add cold water to cover by 3 inches. Cover the bowl and soak the beans in the refrigerator for 8 hours or overnight.

2 Drain the beans and place them in a slow cooker. Add 4 cups of the broth, cover with the lid, and turn the cooker to the low setting.

3 Meanwhile, in a large skillet set over medium heat, warm the oil. When it begins to shimmer, add the bacon and cook for 3 minutes. Then add the onion and cook for 2 minutes. Add the garlic, dry mustard, molasses, orange zest, thyme, and remaining 2 cups broth. Cook for 10 minutes. Add the bacon mixture to the beans, cover with the lid, and cook on the low setting for 6 to 8 hours, until the beans are cooked to your liking. Season with salt to taste, and eat them up.

Spanish Rice

SLOW COOKER SIZE: **4+ QUARTS**
SERVES **6 TO 8 AS A SIDE**
PREP TIME: **5 TO 10 MINUTES**
COOK TIME: **2 HOURS**

You can make the Spanish rice that comes in that yellow bag at the grocery store, or you can make it from scratch in your slow cooker. I implore you to do the latter. I command you.

2 tablespoons unsalted butter

½ cup finely diced onion

1 garlic clove, minced

2 cups long-grain rice

1 teaspoon saffron threads

Kosher salt

1 Melt the butter in a medium skillet set over medium heat. When it begins to bubble and froth, add the onion and cook for 3 minutes. Add the garlic and cook for 2 minutes. Add the rice and the saffron threads, and cook for 2 minutes more, stirring. Transfer the contents of the skillet to a slow cooker. Add 3 cups of cold water, cover with the lid, and cook on the low setting for 2 hours.

2 Gently fluff the rice with a fork, season it with salt to taste, and serve.

Yellow-Eyed Beans with Chorizo & Hard-Boiled Egg

SLOW COOKER SIZE: **4+ QUARTS**
SERVES **4 TO 6**
PREP TIME: **OVERNIGHT SOAK PLUS 10 MINUTES**
COOK TIME: **6 TO 8 HOURS**

This recipe is an ode to Spain, with the earthiness of chorizo, the mystique of smoked paprika, and the utter simplicity of a hard-boiled egg garnish.

My favorite yellow-eyed beans come from Rancho Gordo, a wonderful heirloom bean seller based in California. You can buy them, along with an amazing array of other heritage beans, at select markets and at ranchogordo.com.

1 pound yellow-eyed beans

1 large sweet onion, large-diced

4 garlic cloves, thinly sliced

1 quart Slow Cooker Chicken Broth (page 17)

Kosher salt

1 pound Spanish chorizo, sliced into ¼-inch-thick rounds

2 medium green bell peppers, large-diced

3 tablespoons sweet smoked paprika

1 teaspoon saffron threads

1 cup chopped fresh parsley stems

6 large eggs, hard-boiled

1   Place the beans in a large bowl and add cold water to cover by 3 inches. Cover the bowl and soak the beans in the refrigerator for 8 hours or overnight.

2   Drain the beans and place them in a slow cooker. Add the onion, garlic, and broth. If the beans are not covered with 2 inches of liquid, add enough water to do so. Cover the slow cooker with the lid, turn it to the low setting, and cook for 5 to 7 hours, until the beans are tender to the bite but not busting open. They will continue to cook, mingling with other flavors for another hour, so take that into consideration.

3   Add salt to taste (remembering that the chorizo will bring some salt too), the chorizo, and the bell peppers to the beans and cook on the low setting for 1 hour.

4   To finish, add the paprika, saffron, and parsley stems to the beans and stir well. Season with additional salt, if desired. Grate the hard-boiled eggs. Spoon the stew into individual bowls and garnish each portion with grated egg.

SOUPS

Soups epitomize nourishment, warmth, and a gentle embrace of sustenance. Plus, you usually make too much, and that bounty goes far during the week by providing meals without further labor. With the addition of a simple salad, a wedge of cheese, and some bread, soup makes a fulfilling meal.

The recipes in this chapter run through the vast world of flavors, showing the amazing range of soup styles from around the globe. Everyone likes a good soup, no matter where they lay their head at night.

Soups work well in slow cookers because there is virtually no risk of scorching the bottom, a common and ruinous mishap in stovetop soup cooking.

Soups freeze well, so don't be afraid to make large batches to keep in the freezer for a rainy day. That said, soup will keep well in the fridge for up to five days, on average—and plenty of soups just taste better the next day, anyhow.

P.S. The Chicken Soup with Chiles, Coconut Milk, and Lime is really not to be missed.

Duck & Andouille Gumbo

Slow cookers work well for the long cook time of a gumbo. Don't rush it. And have a beer as you are cooking. That beer is kind of important to complete the lazy Sunday effect that I am envisioning with this gumbo, as that is what gumbo is: a slow cook, often using the abundance of the hunt, or the dock, or the farm. Gumbo is emotive and fulfilling and a way of life when you get really good at it. Don't have a duck? Use a chicken. It's gumbo—it has few rules. Oh, wait, it does have one rule: serve it with steamy white rice. (*See photograph on page 61.*)

1 whole duck (4 to 5 pounds)

Kosher salt and freshly ground black pepper

¼ teaspoon ground cayenne pepper

½ teaspoon sweet smoked paprika

½ teaspoon ground coriander

¼ teaspoon ground cinnamon

¼ teaspoon ground allspice

½ cup plus 1 tablespoon canola oil

2 quarts Slow Cooker Chicken Broth (page 17)

½ cup all-purpose flour

1 large sweet onion, minced

6 garlic cloves, minced

2 celery stalks, minced

1 poblano pepper, seeded and minced

1 red bell pepper, seeded and minced

2 tablespoons chopped fresh thyme leaves

2 cups peeled and diced tomatoes (see page 95)

3 bay leaves

1 pound Andouille sausage, large-diced

½ pound okra, thinly sliced

1 tablespoon Worcestershire sauce

3 cups hot cooked white rice, for serving

1 tablespoon filé powder

Hot sauce, for serving

(recipe continues)

1   Butcher the duck as described on page 133 for chicken, but remove the skin from the breast and keep the breast meat whole.

2   Season the duck thighs and drumsticks all over with 1 teaspoon salt and ½ teaspoon black pepper. In a small bowl, mix together the cayenne, paprika, coriander, cinnamon, and allspice. Liberally season the dark-meat duck pieces with half of this spice mixture.

3   Preheat the oven to 400°F.

4   Heat a large ovenproof skillet over medium-low heat, and add the 1 tablespoon canola oil. Place the duck thighs and drumsticks in the skillet, skin-side down, and slowly render off the fat and crisp the skin, about 30 minutes. Then turn the pieces over, transfer the skillet to the oven, and roast the duck for 30 minutes. Remove the duck pieces and let them come to room temperature on a cooling rack. Strain the duck fat that has rendered off and use it for something else, like duck-fat-roasted taters.

5   Thinly slice the raw duck breasts against the grain. Season the breast meat with salt, pepper, and a touch of the remaining spice mix. Combine the duck breasts and the thighs and drumsticks in a slow cooker and turn it to the high setting. Add the broth to the cooker, cover with the lid, and cook for 1 hour.

6   Let's make a roux: In a large cast-iron pan, heat the remaining ½ cup canola oil over medium-high heat. When the oil is hot, whisk in the flour and season it with a pinch of salt. Change your tool to a wooden spoon and cook, stirring often, until the roux is a beautiful mahogany color—this can take anywhere from 15 to 45 minutes, depending on the heat output of your burner. (As a displaced Canadian not raised in gumbo culture, I used to make my roux way too blond, resulting in a way too lightly flavored gumbo. Make it dark. You'll thank me later.)

7   Once the roux is the color you (I) want, add the onion and cook for 1 minute, stirring constantly. Add the garlic and cook for another 30 seconds. Add the remaining spice mix, and then add the roux to the slow cooker. Add the celery, poblano, bell pepper, thyme, tomatoes, and bay leaves to the cooker, cover with the lid, and cook on the high setting for 3 hours.

8   Add the Andouille, okra, and Worcestershire to the slow cooker, season with salt and pepper, cover with the lid, and cook for 30 minutes. Then ladle the gumbo over steaming hot rice in individual bowls, garnishing each serving with several dashes of filé powder. Serve hot sauce on the side.

Apple–Butternut Squash Soup

SLOW COOKER SIZE: **6+ QUARTS**
SERVES **10 TO 12**
PREP TIME: **15 MINUTES**
COOK TIME: **6 HOURS**

Each fall we get a lot of butternut squash in our local CSA (community supported agriculture) box from Woodland Gardens, a bucolic farm outside of town. The weekly box with a vast array of vegetables and fruits is a delight to guide our home menus, but sometimes we have to be pretty inventive to motor through it all, and one of those items in abundance is always butternut squash. This is the simplest recipe for making something with that bounty, and the apples and squash just work so well together, a tryst of fall flavors.

¼ cup (½ stick) unsalted butter

1 large sweet onion, medium-diced

2 celery stalks, medium-diced

4 red apples, cored and thinly sliced (skins left on)

2 large butternut squash (3 to 4 pounds each), peeled, seeded, and diced

2 bay leaves

4 sprigs fresh thyme

2 quarts Vegetable Stock (page 27) or Slow Cooker Chicken Broth (page 17)

1 teaspoon freshly ground black pepper

1 teaspoon caraway seeds

Kosher salt

Freshly squeezed lemon juice, to taste

½ cup mascarpone cheese

1 teaspoon Aleppo chile flakes or smoked paprika

2 tablespoons thinly sliced scallions (white and light green parts only)

1   Place the butter in a 6-quart or larger slow cooker and warm it on the high setting for at least 15 minutes.

2   Add the onion, celery, apples, squash, bay leaves, thyme sprigs, stock, pepper, caraway, and 1 tablespoon salt to the slow cooker, cover with the lid, and cook on the high setting for 6 hours.

3   Remove the bay leaves and thyme sprigs. Carefully transfer the soup, in batches, to a blender or food processor and puree until smooth. (You could also use an immersion blender.) If you want a super-smooth consistency, pass the puree through a fine-mesh sieve or strainer. Season the soup with more salt and a squeeze of lemon juice, to taste. Portion the soup into individual bowls and garnish each one with a dollop of mascarpone, a sprinkle of Aleppo, and a smattering of scallions.

Tortilla Soup

I have a friend named Homero. Homero started working for me when he was about nineteen. He is a strong person, emotionally and physically. He taught me many things in his years in my employ, especially about the region of Mexico he is from, Michoacán. Homero used to make this traditional soup for family (staff) meal at my restaurant 5&10, and then it became a staple of the menu for a while, because it is just that good.

1 whole chicken (3 to 4 pounds)

3 tablespoons extra-virgin olive oil

1 medium onion, small-diced

1 celery stalk, small-diced

3 garlic cloves, minced

1 cup vegetable oil

4 white corn tortillas

2 dried pasilla chiles, stemmed, seeded, and cut into small pieces

3 pounds heirloom tomatoes, peeled (see page 95)

Kosher salt

2 quarts Slow Cooker Chicken Broth (page 17)

1 (15-ounce) can hominy, drained and rinsed

¼ cup freshly squeezed lime juice, plus lime wedges for serving

½ cup minced fresh cilantro leaves and stems

2 avocados

¾ cup Mexican crema

1 Butcher the chicken into 2 wings, 2 thighs, 2 drumsticks, and 2 breast halves (see page 133).

2 Place a large skillet over medium heat and warm 2 tablespoons of the olive oil in it. When the oil is shimmering, add the chicken pieces, skin-side down (this can be done in batches, if necessary). Crisp the chicken for 10 minutes, then flip the pieces over and cook for 3 minutes on the other side. Transfer the chicken to a paper towel–lined plate to drain.

3 Place the skillet back over medium heat and add the remaining 1 tablespoon olive oil. When the oil is shimmering, add the onion and sweat it for 5 minutes, until soft. Then add the celery and garlic and cook for another 3 minutes, until softened. Remove the pan from the heat.

4 Heat the vegetable oil in a separate 10-inch skillet over medium heat. When the oil is shimmering but not smoking (about 350°F), fry the tortillas, in batches, until golden brown; as they are cooked, set them aside to drain on paper towels. Leave the oil in the skillet, letting it cool a bit. When they are cool, break the tortillas into pieces.

(recipe continues)

5   Add the pasilla pieces to the slightly cooled oil and fry them very briefly over medium heat until toasted, about 10 seconds. Remove them with a slotted spoon and drain on paper towels.

6   Cut the peeled tomatoes in half and gently squeeze out the seeds with your hand. Coarsely chop the seeded halves. In a blender or food processor, puree the pasillas and tomatoes together. Season with a pinch of salt.

7   Place the chicken pieces, tomato-pasilla puree, and sautéed vegetables in a slow cooker. Add the broth, cover with the lid, and cook on the low setting for 4 hours.

8   Remove the chicken pieces from the cooker and let them cool. Meanwhile, stir the hominy into the remaining ingredients in the slow cooker, cover, and cook for 15 minutes. When the chicken is cool enough to handle, remove the skin and pull the meat off the bones; discard the skin and bones. Shred the meat and return it to the slow cooker. Stir in the lime juice, half of the cilantro, and salt to taste. Halve the avocados, remove the seed, scoop out the flesh, and slice. Serve in individual bowls, finish each bowl with ample avocado, and offer the fried tortillas, crema, remaining cilantro, and lime wedges as garnishes.

Lentil Soup with Kale & Sour Cream

SLOW COOKER SIZE: **4+ QUARTS**

SERVES **6**

PREP TIME: **15 MINUTES**

COOK TIME: **3 HOURS PLUS 10 MINUTES FOR FINISHING**

I love lentils. They cook quickly, are incredibly nutritious, are inexpensive, and have a culinary dexterity about them—nutty and meaty-tasting, they go with many flavors and are staples around the world. We just don't use them enough on this continent.

Traditionally, lentil soup is about a 4:1 ratio of liquid to lentils, but you can make it as brothy as you wish. I prefer to use regular green lentils here, but if you want to get fancy you could also use du Puy lentils, the small dark green lentil of France, or even black beluga lentils; but I would avoid Indian red dal lentils, as they tend to break down too much for a soup like this.

Matched with a piece of toasted baguette, this hearty classic soup makes a fine meal.

2 quarts Vegetable Stock (page 27)

2 tablespoons extra-virgin olive oil

2 shallots, minced

1 large carrot, finely diced

2 celery stalks, finely diced

2 sprigs fresh thyme

1 tablespoon sweet smoked paprika

1 tablespoon coriander seeds, toasted and ground

1 pound green lentils

Kosher salt

2 tablespoons unsalted butter

4 cups chopped stemmed Red Russian kale (½-inch squares)

1 teaspoon grated lemon zest

1 tablespoon sherry vinegar

Sour cream, for serving

Chopped fresh flat-leaf parsley leaves, for serving

1 Turn a slow cooker to the high setting, add the vegetable stock, and heat it, covered, until warm (this may take 15 minutes).

2 Place a medium sauté pan over medium heat. Add the olive oil. When it begins to shimmer, add the shallots and cook for 2 minutes, or until translucent. Add the carrot and celery and cook for 2 more minutes, until they are starting to soften. Add the thyme sprigs, smoked paprika, and ground coriander. Stir well and transfer the mixture to the slow cooker.

3 Rinse the lentils in a fine-mesh sieve under cold running water. Add them to the slow cooker. Add 2 teaspoons salt, or to taste, cover with the lid, and cook on the high setting for 3 hours, or until the lentils are tender and the flavors have melded.

4 Remove the thyme sprigs. Use a ladle to transfer 1 cup of the soup to a blender; puree it, then return the puree to the slow cooker.

(Alternatively, take an immersion blender and quickly buzz the soup a bit to make it a little smoother and bring it together.)

5 Place a large skillet over medium-high heat and add the butter. When the butter bubbles and froths, add the kale and cook, stirring, for about 2 minutes, until it has wilted.

Season with a pinch of salt and add the kale to the soup. Add the lemon zest and sherry vinegar, and season to taste with salt. Soup is done! Bowl it up or chill it down; pack it up, and save it for later. When serving, garnish each bowl with a dollop of sour cream and a sprinkle of parsley.

Oxtail & Barley Soup

SLOW COOKER SIZE: **6+ QUARTS**
SERVES **4 TO 6**
PREP TIME: **25 MINUTES**
COOK TIME: **8 HOURS**

Oxtails aren't the most common cut of beef, and they're sadly underappreciated. They have a lot of connective tissue that melts away as it cooks, revealing a rich meat that is wonderfully silky. This soup makes me think of cold nights at a cabin in Canada, a fire in the hearth, and a blanket on my lap—the beef is deep and mellow and the barley cooks to a thick, rich consistency. Make sure you buy pearled barley, because unpearled barley takes a much longer time to cook.

3 pounds oxtails

Kosher salt and freshly ground black pepper

3 tablespoons olive oil

4 leeks (white and light green parts), halved lengthwise, rinsed well, and sliced into ½-inch-thick rounds

1 celery stalk, small-diced, leaves reserved

3 garlic cloves, thinly sliced

1 large tomato

1 quart Beef Shin Stock (page 21)

2 cups dry red wine

4 sprigs fresh thyme

2 bay leaves

2 cups pearled barley

1 teaspoon coriander seeds, toasted and ground

1 large parsnip, peeled and small-diced (1 cup)

1   Preheat a slow cooker on the low setting for at least 20 minutes.

2   Pat the oxtails dry and season them well with salt and 1 tablespoon black pepper.

3   Heat the olive oil in a large skillet over medium heat. When the oil is shimmering, sear the oxtails for 3 minutes on each meaty side until nicely browned, a total of about 12 minutes. Transfer the oxtails to a paper towel–lined plate to drain. Add the leeks, celery, and garlic to the hot skillet and cook over medium heat for 5 minutes; then set aside.

4   Heat a small skillet, preferably cast iron, over medium-high heat. Slice the tomato in half and place each half in the skillet, cut-side down. Cook for 5 minutes to develop a good bit of char. Remove from the heat.

5   Add the oxtails, leeks, celery, and garlic, tomato halves, stock, wine, thyme sprigs, and bay leaves to the slow cooker. Cover with the lid and cook on the low setting for 6 hours.

6   Remove the oxtails and put them in the refrigerator to cool. When they are cool enough to handle, pull the meat apart, discarding any bone, skin, fat, and tough sinew.

7   Add the oxtail meat, barley, coriander, and ½ teaspoon black pepper to the slow cooker. Stir to combine; then cover with the lid and cook on the low setting for another 2 hours. When you are 30 minutes from the finish line, add the diced parsnip. Before serving, season the soup to taste with salt and pepper.

8   Remove the bay leaves and thyme sprigs from the cooker. Serve the soup directly out of the cooker pot at the table, or if you prefer, ladle it into individual bowls and garnish with the reserved celery leaves.

Butter Bean Minestrone

SLOW COOKER SIZE: **4+ QUARTS**
SERVES **6**
PREP TIME: **OVERNIGHT SOAK PLUS 30 MINUTES**
COOK TIME: **7 TO 9 HOURS**

Southern minestrone at its finest is a brothy celebration of all things vegetable, with a bright basil pistou stirred in to finish. You can tweak this recipe to use whatever you have in the crisper drawer. Remember that minestrone, like many soups, tastes better the next day, heated up and served with good crusty bread and some cheese on the side.

1 pound dried butter beans

¼ cup extra-virgin olive oil

2 medium sweet onions, small-diced

2 quarts Vegetable Stock (page 27) or Slow Cooker Chicken Broth (page 17)

1 large carrot, small-diced

1 celery stalk, small-diced

1 teaspoon freshly ground fennel seeds

4 plum tomatoes, small-diced

1 small zucchini, small-diced

1 teaspoon freshly ground black pepper

Kosher salt

1 cup Basil Pistou (recipe follows)

1 Place the beans in a large bowl and add cold water to cover by 3 inches. Cover the bowl and soak the beans in the refrigerator overnight.

2 The next day, in a medium skillet over medium heat, warm 2 tablespoons of the olive oil. When the oil is shimmering, add the onions and sauté for 5 minutes, or until softening, then remove from the heat.

3 Drain the beans and add them to the slow cooker. Add the stock, onions, carrot, and celery. Cover with the lid, turn to the low setting, and cook for 6 to 8 hours, until the beans are tender but not busted.

4 Stir the ground fennel, tomatoes, zucchini, pepper, and 1 tablespoon salt into the beans. Cover with the lid and cook for 1 hour more. Season to taste with additional salt.

5 Ladle the soup into individual bowls and garnish each one with Basil Pistou and a drizzle of the remaining olive oil. Serve and eat!

BASIL PISTOU

Basil pistou is great to spread on crostini or to dollop on grilled meat or poached fish, and delicious layered into your favorite lasagna recipe. The possibilities are endless!

MAKES ABOUT 2 CUPS

Kosher salt

2 cups lightly packed fresh basil leaves

½ cup grated Parmigiano-Reggiano cheese

½ cup shelled roasted unsalted pistachios

½ cup olive oil

Freshly ground black pepper

1   Fill a large saucepan with water and bring it to a boil. Fill a large bowl with ice and cold water and set it nearby.

2   Add 1 teaspoon salt to the boiling water. Blanch the basil in the boiling water for about 20 seconds, until it develops a bright green color, and then immediately plunge it into the waiting ice bath. After a minute, strain the basil from the water, wrap it in a kitchen towel, and squeeze gently to remove excess water.

3   Place the basil, Parmigiano-Reggiano, and pistachios in a food processor and turn it on. Slowly drizzle in the olive oil. Season to taste with salt and pepper. Refrigerate, covered, until ready to use. The pistou will keep in the fridge for about 1 week.

Ribollita

SLOW COOKER SIZE: **6+ QUARTS**

SERVES **8**

PREP TIME: **OVERNIGHT SOAK PLUS 35 MINUTES**

COOK TIME: **4 HOURS, THEN ANOTHER 3 HOURS**

Ribollita is like a heartier version of minestrone, thickened with bread and redolent with garlic. It is a beautiful soup when it's fresh from the pot, but it is also perhaps the most noble of leftovers. I like to take a ladleful of soup and reheat it in a hot pan with a little olive oil. When the moisture cooks down, it almost becomes an Italian bean pancake, luscious and just a touch crisp. This is a blatant rip-off, respectfully, of a version I had at Craig Stoll's Delfina twenty years ago. It was a rainy San Francisco night and we were wedged into one of the tiny tables in the tiny restaurant, the first place that I had ever been to where they told you, upon sitting, what time they needed you to leave in order to accommodate the next reservation. Fortunately this strange instruction was totally compensated by amazingly tender and sensuous food, and we ended up loving every moment of it. We also left on time.

1 pound dried cannellini beans

2 tablespoons extra-virgin olive oil

1 large sweet onion, small-diced

Kosher salt

2 large carrots, small-diced

3 celery stalks, small-diced

½ large butternut squash, peeled and small-diced (2 cups)

1 head garlic, cloves separated, peeled, and thinly sliced

1 (28-ounce) can San Marzano tomatoes, drained

Bouquet garni: 2 bay leaves plus a couple sprigs each of fresh sage, oregano, flat-leaf parsley, and thyme, tied together with twine

1 tablespoon crushed red pepper flakes

1 pound cavolo nero (a.k.a. dinosaur kale or Tuscan kale), leaves torn into small pieces, stems finely minced

3 cups torn country bread, toasted

1½ cups finely grated Parmigiano-Reggiano cheese

(recipe continues)

Chicken Soup with Chiles, Coconut Milk & Lime

SLOW COOKER SIZE: **4+ QUARTS**
SERVES **4**
PREP TIME: **20 MINUTES**
COOK TIME: **4 HOURS**

I love the flavors of Thai food. Redolent with ginger, fish sauce, scallions, and lime, luxuriant in coconut milk, and fresh with mint and cilantro, it is a full-flavored cuisine. This recipe borrows a lot of that sensibility and translates it into a simple soup that is nourishing, spicy, and just downright tasty.

4 bone-in, skin-on chicken thighs

Kosher salt

1 tablespoon vegetable oil

2 shallots, minced

2 tablespoons minced fresh ginger

2 tablespoons minced lemongrass, from the tender, pale inner layers (use the bottom 4 inches or so, from 1 or 2 stalks)

1 teaspoon red curry paste

2 Thai (bird's-eye) chiles, minced

2 cups thinly sliced stemmed fresh shiitake mushrooms (½ pound)

1½ quarts Slow Cooker Chicken Broth (page 17)

2 tablespoons fish sauce

1 (14-ounce) can coconut milk

2 tablespoons freshly squeezed lime juice

Thinly sliced carrot rounds, for garnish

Thinly sliced scallions (white and light green parts only), for garnish

Fresh cilantro leaves, for garnish

Torn fresh mint leaves, for garnish

1   Pat the chicken thighs dry and season them well with salt. Place a large skillet over medium heat and add the vegetable oil. When the oil is shimmering, add the chicken thighs, skin-side down, and cook for about 10 minutes, until they are very well browned. Flip the thighs over and brown them for 3 minutes on the other side. Transfer the chicken to a plate.

2   Raise the heat under the skillet to high and add the shallots, ginger, and lemongrass to the pan. Cook for 1 minute, until fragrant, then add the curry paste, chiles, shiitakes, and 1 teaspoon salt. Cook for 2 minutes. Then pour the contents of the skillet into the slow cooker and turn the setting to low.

3   Add the chicken broth and fish sauce to the cooker, then add the chicken thighs. Cover with the lid and cook on the low setting for 4 hours.

4   Remove the lid and stir in the coconut milk and lime juice. Add salt to taste. Portion the soup into individual bowls, making sure to allocate a piece of chicken to each one. Serve the soup with the carrot rounds, scallions, cilantro, and mint alongside.

VEGETABLE-FOCUSED

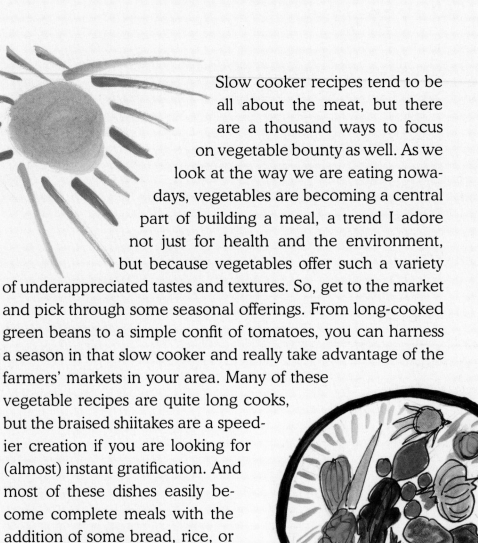

Slow cooker recipes tend to be all about the meat, but there are a thousand ways to focus on vegetable bounty as well. As we look at the way we are eating nowadays, vegetables are becoming a central part of building a meal, a trend I adore not just for health and the environment, but because vegetables offer such a variety of underappreciated tastes and textures. So, get to the market and pick through some seasonal offerings. From long-cooked green beans to a simple confit of tomatoes, you can harness a season in that slow cooker and really take advantage of the farmers' markets in your area. Many of these vegetable recipes are quite long cooks, but the braised shiitakes are a speedier creation if you are looking for (almost) instant gratification. And most of these dishes easily become complete meals with the addition of some bread, rice, or pasta on the side. I just want you to eat your vegetables and enjoy the seasons.

Boiled Peanuts

"Green" peanuts are the raw peanut, before curing and roasting. They have a season that runs from August to November, but it can be challenging to find them north of Virginia. Still, you *should* make the effort to find them, because they are an amazing snack when boiled until soft—like beans with a rich, nutty flavor—in water that's spiked with vinegar and red pepper. (Try looking in the produce section of Asian markets, or buy the green peanuts online.) When we cook them, we end up giving them to friends and neighbors—it's a natural way of demonstrating that innate Southern hospitality. And if you like a little kick to your nuts, add some cayenne to the mix before cooking them.

2 pounds green peanuts

½ cup kosher salt

½ cup cider vinegar

1 tablespoon crushed red pepper flakes

1   Using the lid of the slow cooker as a stencil, trace the outline onto a piece of parchment paper with a pencil. Cut out the shape with scissors and set it aside.

2   Place the peanuts, salt, vinegar, and red pepper flakes in a slow cooker and add 4 quarts of water. Cover with the lid and cook on the high setting for 1 hour. Then place the piece of parchment directly on the peanuts, reduce the setting to low, and cook for 11 hours, or until the peanuts are tender, like well-cooked beans. Serve them warm, or cool the peanuts in their cooking liquid and store them in it too. They will keep in the refrigerator for up to 1 week.

HOW TO PREPARE AN ARTICHOKE

1   Prepare a bowl of cold water with 1 teaspoon of fresh lemon juice added.

2   Using a paring knife, remove the skin from the stem of the artichoke, leaving
the stem intact. With a serrated knife, remove the top ½ inch to 2 inches of the
artichoke (depending on how big it is) to expose the tender interior leaves. Snap
off the tough outer leaves. Then, using the serrated knife, slice the artichoke in half
from stem to top. Using the paring knife, cut into the heart-pith juncture. It looks a
bit like fuzz. Cut away the inner fuzzy part (it's called the choke), being careful not
to cut through the meaty part underneath (that is the heart—the delicious tender
part that we want to keep). Submerge the artichoke halves in the lemon water until
you are ready to cook them, to prevent discoloration.

Artichoke & Carrot Barigoule

SLOW COOKER SIZE: **6+ QUARTS**
SERVES **6 TO 8 AS A SIDE**
PREP TIME: **40 MINUTES**
COOK TIME: **2 TO 3 HOURS**

Barigoule is a foundational recipe from the South of France that quickly makes you realize why the flavors of Provence are held in such high culinary esteem. In this version, garlic, olive oil, bay leaf, and lemon create an acidic braise for the artichokes, providing a foil to their natural richness, with the butter giving luxury and finesse. It is a keeper of a recipe.

2 tablespoons olive oil

1 large sweet onion, small-diced

3 garlic cloves, thinly sliced

Kosher salt

12 globe artichokes, cleaned and prepped (see opposite)

1 cup freshly squeezed lemon juice

10 small carrots, halved lengthwise, greens removed

4 bay leaves

1 cup dry white wine

2 tablespoons unsalted butter

2 tablespoons chopped fresh flat-leaf parsley leaves

1 Using the lid of your slow cooker as a stencil, trace the outline onto a piece of parchment paper with a pencil. Cut out the shape with scissors and set it aside.

2 Turn the slow cooker to the high setting and add the olive oil, onion, garlic, and 1 teaspoon salt. Cook, stirring occasionally, for 30 minutes, or until soft. Add the artichokes, lemon juice, and 4 cups water, along with the carrots, bay leaves, and white wine. Cover the contents of the cooker with the cut-out piece of parchment, to keep the artichokes fully immersed, and then cover with the lid. Turn the setting to low and cook for 2 to 3 hours, until the artichokes and carrots are fork-tender.

3 Using a slotted spoon, transfer the vegetables to a large mixing bowl. Add ½ cup of the cooking liquid, the butter, and the parsley, and toss. Season with more salt, if desired, and serve immediately in a bowl or deep platter.

Southern-Style Green Beans

SLOW COOKER SIZE: **4+ QUARTS**
SERVES **4 AS A SIDE**
PREP TIME: **20 MINUTES**
COOK TIME: **4 HOURS**

Long-cooked vegetables are sometimes utterly beautiful things, and this recipe is my go-to for convincing young chefs that long cooks on green things can result in stunning flavors. In cooking school, students are yelled at for vegetables that look anything other than bright green, but cooking these green beans until camouflage colored and soft makes them nutty and sweet. Let 'em go.

1 pound fresh green beans

¼ pound slab or thick-cut bacon, small-diced

1 medium sweet onion, small-diced

4 garlic cloves, minced

¼ cup cider vinegar

½ teaspoon crushed red pepper flakes

2 sprigs fresh thyme

1 cup Slow Cooker Chicken Broth (page 17)

1 tablespoon cane syrup

Kosher salt

1 Preheat a slow cooker on the low setting for 20 minutes.

2 Meanwhile, trim the green beans. Rinse them well and place them on paper towels to dry.

3 Place a medium skillet over medium heat. Add the bacon and cook for 10 minutes, or until it is mostly cooked and most of the fat has rendered. Add the onion and garlic and cook for 5 minutes, or until softened. Add the vinegar, red pepper flakes, and thyme sprigs. Bring to a boil and cook for 1 minute to reduce the vinegar slightly; then remove the pan from heat.

4 Place the green beans in the slow cooker, add the bacon mixture, broth, cane syrup, and 1 tablespoon salt, and cook on the low setting for 4 hours. Remove the thyme sprigs and discard them. Season with additional salt, if desired, and serve the beans in a bowl or deep platter, with some of the cooking juices poured over the top.

Slow Cooker Collard Greens

SLOW COOKER SIZE: **6+ QUARTS**
SERVES **6 TO 8 AS A HEARTY SIDE**
PREP TIME: **30 MINUTES**
COOK TIME: **5 TO 7 HOURS**

I like to think the slow cooker was invented by a Southern home cook. Collards can sit in there for hours on end, breaking down as they should, the liquid turning into pot likker, the residual elixir of greens cookery that is like culinary platinum in the South. The wonderful aroma of collards cooking both excites my palate and calms my anxieties.

2 pounds fresh collard greens

3 ounces skin-on fatback, rinsed and cut into large chunks

1 medium sweet onion, minced

1 garlic clove, minced

⅓ cup cider vinegar

⅓ cup sorghum molasses

1 teaspoon crushed red pepper flakes

Kosher salt

1 Preheat a slow cooker on the high setting for at least 15 minutes.

2 Fill the sink with cold water. Tear the collard leaves from their spines and into bite-size pieces, and submerge the pieces in the cold water. Thinly slice the spines against the grain. Add the sliced spines to the collard leaves.

3 Place a large skillet over medium heat and add the fatback. Cook for 5 minutes, or until some of the fat has rendered. Add the onion and cook for 3 minutes, until translucent.

Empty the fatback and onion into the slow cooker. Using a slotted spoon or a mesh skimmer, scoop the collard leaves and spines from the water and place them in the slow cooker. Add the garlic, vinegar, molasses, red pepper flakes, and 1 teaspoon salt. Add 2 cups of water and stir as best you can to combine the ingredients. Cover with the lid and cook on the high setting for 1 hour. Stir the ingredients (to ensure even cooking), re-cover the slow cooker, reduce the setting to low, and cook for 4 to 6 hours, until the collards are well broken down but not mushy. Season with salt to taste.

4 The collards can be eaten immediately, served with the pot likker. Or they can be cooled and kept in the refrigerator for up to 4 days, a quick reheat away from a great side dish. You can also freeze cooked collards with their pot likker for up to 6 months. If you like them on the drier side, drain the pot likker from the collards—but be sure to drink that likker up. Likker Elixir: it keeps sickness at bay.

Chickpea & Eggplant Stew

SLOW COOKER SIZE: **4+ QUARTS**

SERVES **4 TO 6**

PREP TIME: **OVERNIGHT SOAK PLUS 35 MINUTES**

COOK TIME: **2 HOURS**

Rich fried eggplant, nearly melted with peppers, herbs, and spices, forms the base of this stew, studded with creamy chickpeas. This is a great dish to have ready in the fridge. It makes a quick meal with rice and some hot sauce, and it freezes well, too. Dried chickpeas are far less expensive and yield better results than canned, so get used to soaking things overnight. When shopping for dried beans, most any will do, but try to find a shop that moves a lot of them . . . think a Mexican or Indian grocery store, cultures that revel in their beans and dried legumes. New-crop beans, though dry like old ones, cook up much more quickly, and usually with better texture and flavor than years-old beans.

½ pound dried chickpeas

1 globe eggplant (about 1 pound)

½ cup olive oil, or more as needed

1 large sweet onion, minced

1 poblano chile, seeded and finely diced

1 red bell pepper, seeded and finely diced

6 garlic cloves, minced

1 pound ripe fresh tomatoes, diced

½ cup finely minced fresh cilantro stems

1 tablespoon minced fresh oregano leaves

½ teaspoon coriander seeds, toasted and ground

½ teaspoon cumin seeds, toasted and ground

2 bay leaves

1 cup Vegetable Stock (page 27)

Kosher salt

½ cup crumbled feta cheese

¼ cup fresh cilantro leaves, for garnish

1   Place the chickpeas in a large bowl and add cold water to cover by 3 inches. Cover the bowl and let soak in the refrigerator overnight.

2   Drain the chickpeas and pour them into a large pot. Add enough fresh water to cover them by 2 inches and bring to a boil. Simmer for 30 minutes. Skim the flotsam of white bubbly stuff and discard. Drain the chickpeas and set them aside.

3   Meanwhile, preheat a slow cooker on the high setting for at least 15 minutes. Peel the eggplant and cut it into 1-inch dice.

4   Place a very large skillet over medium-high heat and add the olive oil. When the oil is shimmering, add the eggplant, in batches, and fry on all sides until evenly browned, about 2 minutes. Don't crowd the pan, or you will steam the eggplant instead of frying it. As it finishes browning, transfer the eggplant to a paper towel–lined plate to drain. Add more olive oil to the pan as needed to evenly brown all of the eggplant pieces.

5   Still over medium-high heat, add the onion, poblano, and bell pepper to the skillet. Cook, stirring every minute or so, for 5 minutes or until softened. Add the garlic and cook for another 2 minutes. Remove the skillet from the heat and set it aside.

6   Place the chickpeas, eggplant, and onion mixture in the slow cooker. Add the tomato, cilantro stems, oregano, coriander, cumin, bay leaves, and stock. Stir well. Season with 1 teaspoon salt, cover with the lid, and cook on the high setting for 2 hours. If you see the bay leaves, remove them and discard; otherwise just know the Heimlich maneuver.

7   Season the stew to taste with salt, and serve it in a soup tureen with the feta and cilantro leaves alongside, or spoon the soup into individual bowls and garnish each one with feta and cilantro before serving.

Butter-Braised Cabbage

SLOW COOKER SIZE: **4+ QUARTS**
SERVES **6 TO 8 AS A SIDE**
PREP TIME: **15 MINUTES**
COOK TIME: **4 HOURS**

Cabbage is inexpensive, yet awesome. Braising it gently in butter brings out its sweetness, and the caraway gives it a soft floral note. This is a great side dish to serve with any roasted or braised meat, but especially with that corned beef you made (see page 172). So decadent, yet so simple, and so utterly classic.

½ pound (2 sticks) unsalted butter

1 head firm green cabbage (3 to 4 pounds)

1 teaspoon caraway seeds, toasted and ground

2 sprigs fresh thyme

2 cups Slow Cooker Chicken Broth (page 17)

Kosher salt

1 tablespoon cider vinegar

½ cup chopped fresh flat-leaf parsley leaves

1   Add the butter to a slow cooker and heat it on the high setting for 15 minutes, or until the butter has melted fully.

2   Meanwhile, cut the cabbage in half lengthwise, and then cut out the core. Cut each half into approximately 1-inch cubes.

3   Add the cabbage, caraway, thyme sprigs, and broth to the slow cooker. Season with 1 teaspoon salt, stir well to combine, and then cover with the lid and cook on the high setting for 3 hours.

4   Reduce the setting to low, remove the lid, and add 1 teaspoon salt, the vinegar, and the parsley to the cabbage. Stir to combine, re-cover the cooker, and cook on the low setting for 1 hour. Season to taste with more salt and serve.

Braised Shiitake Mushrooms with Tofu, Thai Basil & Chiles

SLOW COOKER SIZE: **4+ QUARTS**
SERVES **4 TO 6**
PREP TIME: **15 MINUTES**
COOK TIME: **2 HOURS**

This is a recipe for your virtuous meatless Monday. You will be laughing at all the suckers eating dry, lifeless veggie burgers while you dig into the meaty deliciousness of braised shiitakes. Mushrooms braise into delectable morsels with near-meat consistency, and they really could become a staple protein replacement at your table. This is a simple recipe, yet it yields stunning results and makes a nice supper when served with rice.

2 tablespoons red miso paste

¼ cup rice vinegar

3 shallots, sliced into thin rings

2 tablespoons minced fresh ginger

Kosher salt

2 pounds fresh shiitake mushrooms, stems removed, caps left whole

3 Thai (bird's-eye) chiles, seeded and sliced into thin rings

1 small red bell pepper, seeded and thinly sliced

1 small yellow bell pepper, seeded and thinly sliced

½ pound firm tofu, cut into ½-inch-thick planks, seasoned with a pinch of salt and pressed (see below)

¼ cup freshly torn Thai basil leaves

1 Preheat a slow cooker on the high setting for at least 15 minutes.

2 Pour 4 cups of water into the slow cooker. Add the miso, vinegar, shallots, ginger, and ½ teaspoon salt, whisking well to fully dissolve the miso. Then add the mushrooms and Thai chiles, cover with the lid, and cook on the high setting for 1 hour.

3 Add the bell peppers and tofu to the mushroom mixture, re-cover the cooker, and cook for 1 hour more, still on the high setting. To finish, add the basil, mix well, season with salt to taste, and serve in a deep platter or a bowl.

PRESSING TOFU

Tofu has a lot of water in it, so it's often pressed to expel some, leaving you with a denser, chewier, more flavorful bite. At home I just place a big colander in the sink and then find a plate that nestles in it tightly. Cut the tofu into large 1-inch-thick rectangles, arrange them in a single layer in the colander, and place the plate over them. Weight the plate down with a brick or with cans of beans or whatever. An hour later, you have pressed tofu. (You can also press the tofu between two heavy plates in the fridge overnight. This ain't rocket science.)

Spring Stew

SLOW COOKER SIZE: **4+ QUARTS**
SERVES **2 TO 4**
PREP TIME: **1 HOUR OR ABOUT 10 MINUTES, DEPENDING ON COOKING METHOD**
COOK TIME: **3 TO 4 HOURS**

I love this stew—it takes the essence of spring and turns it into a meal. Artichokes, freshly dug potatoes, sugar snap peas, and some Provençal spices all marry in a luxurious braise. Pair it with a nice rosé and enjoy!

¼ pound pancetta, small-diced

1 quart Slow Cooker Chicken Broth (page 17)

2 cups dry white wine

3 tablespoons freshly squeezed lemon juice

Kosher salt

8 medium globe artichokes, cleaned and prepped (see page 88), hearts cut into 1-inch pieces

½ pound new potatoes, scrubbed and sliced into ¼-inch-thick rounds

1 tablespoon ground fennel seeds

½ pound sugar snap peas, rinsed, ends trimmed

2 tablespoons unsalted butter

2 sprigs fresh rosemary, cut into 2-inch lengths

2 tablespoons minced fresh flat-leaf parsley leaves

1 tablespoon Aleppo chile flakes (or dried Urfa chile or crushed red pepper flakes)

1   Preheat a slow cooker on the high setting for at least 20 minutes.

2   In the slow cooker, cook the pancetta for 30 minutes to render some of the fat. Add the broth, wine, lemon juice, and 2 teaspoons salt, and cook for another 30 minutes. (Alternatively, cook the pancetta in a skillet over medium heat for about 5 minutes, add the broth, wine, lemon juice, and salt, and bring the mixture to a simmer; then add it to the cooker.) Add the artichoke hearts, potatoes, and fennel, and cover with the lid. Reduce the setting to low and cook for 3 hours.

3   Uncover the slow cooker and add the snap peas, butter, rosemary, parsley, and Aleppo chile. Stir well, re-cover the cooker, and cook for 10 minutes. Then season the stew with additional salt, if desired. Ladle it into individual bowls or serve it in a tureen.

SEAFOOD

Slow cookers cook things gently, which fish and shellfish love. Low and slow. When investing in seafood, buy it from a source that you trust, a place that moves a lot of product with people who take pride in the shop they run. That could be a large supermarket or a small fishmonger.

Research how the seafood gets to your table as well, as conservancy is a very important issue when it comes to the shrinking bounty of our oceans. When in doubt, check out the Seafood Watch app, an amazing resource put together by the Monterey Bay Aquarium; it focuses your awareness on the seafood that is sustainable, bountiful, and not laden with mercury. These are the smart choices for healthier oceans in the next generation. For me it has become an indispensable resource to guide where my fish dollars are spent.

Southern Shrimp Pilau

SLOW COOKER SIZE: **4+ QUARTS**
SERVES **4 TO 6**
PREP TIME: **40 MINUTES**
COOK TIME: **2½ HOURS**

Shrimp pilau is a Low Country staple, and it should become a staple in your house as well. It's a cousin of jambalaya, or biryani, or even risotto in that it's a gently stewed rice, in this case matched with really great shrimp. While we're on the subject, let's clarify something about great American Gulf or Atlantic shrimp: shrimp freeze well, so don't be afraid to buy a five-pound block of shrimp frozen in salted water. In season, which is spring through late summer, buy them fresh; but out of season, you can rely on that frozen block. (*See photograph on page 104.*)

1 cup white basmati rice

2 tablespoons unsalted butter

1 large sweet onion, small-diced

1 cup small-diced country ham

2 medium yellow bell peppers, small-diced

4 bay leaves

6 sprigs fresh thyme

1½ cups Shrimp Stock (page 24)

½ cup bottled clam juice

1 pound fresh domestic shrimp, peeled, deveined, and tails removed if desired

Kosher salt

1 teaspoon freshly ground black pepper

1½ scallions (white and light green parts only), thinly sliced

½ cup Sun Gold or other cherry tomatoes, halved

Hot sauce, for serving

1   Place the rice in a medium-mesh strainer and rinse it under cold running water to remove the excess starch. Drain well and set aside.

2   In a slow cooker on the high setting, melt the butter until it begins to bubble and froth, about 10 minutes. Add the onion and cook for 10 minutes, until softened. Then add the ham and bell peppers and cook for 10 more minutes. (Alternatively, you can do this in a skillet over medium heat: Cook the onions for 3 minutes, then the ham and peppers for another 3, then place in the slow cooker.) Stir in the rice. Add the bay leaves, thyme sprigs, stock, and clam juice. Cover with the lid, reduce the setting to low, and cook for 2 hours.

3   Season the shrimp with salt, and add them and the black pepper to the slow cooker. Stir, re-cover, and cook for 30 minutes. Remove the bay leaves and thyme sprigs and discard. Spoon the shrimp pilau onto a serving platter or into individual shallow bowls, and garnish with the scallions and tomatoes. Serve the hot sauce on the side.

Catfish Stew

Catfish stew—is it Southern? I mean, what is Southern food? You got six months for a chat over a number of cases of bourbon? There will be some tears and some wrestling of emotions and probably real wrestling, too.

The short of it is that stewed catfish dishes are widely found across western Africa, particularly in Nigeria, and the very similar methods and results of those stews have been around in North America since way before George Washington's parents ever got to first base.

So yes, catfish stew is a Southern recipe because it exists in our history of Southern food. Not to get all serious on you, but many recipes and foodways in the Southern United States exist only because of slavery, something that we need to come to terms with and honor in the right, solemn way. These are recipes that were never meant to be here, yet have become an important part of our cuisine. I just want to make sure that we remember that. Respect.

So go make some food and gather round the table and talk about where all of these flavors come from and what that all means. 'Cause it means a lot to converse about where we have been as a culture, and where we are going.

1 (28-ounce) can Italian plum tomatoes

½ pound slab bacon, small-diced

1 large sweet onion, small-diced

1 large red bell pepper, cored, seeded, and small-diced

1 celery stalk, small-diced

4 garlic cloves, minced

4 whole cloves

1 teaspoon ground mace

1 teaspoon ground allspice

2 cups bottled clam juice

2 cups Fish Stock (page 22) or Vegetable Stock (page 27)

1 pound fingerling potatoes, cut into 1-inch-thick rounds

Kosher salt

2 tablespoons Worcestershire sauce

1 teaspoon hot sauce

1½ pounds catfish fillets, cut into 1-inch pieces

2 tablespoons unsalted butter

¼ cup minced fresh flat-leaf parsley leaves

½ cup store-bought pickled banana peppers

Freshly ground black pepper

(recipe continues)

1 Pour the tomatoes and their liquid into a food processor and pulse to break them down a bit.

2 Set a slow cooker to the high setting. Add the bacon and cook until most of the fat has rendered, 20 to 30 minutes. Add the onion, bell pepper, and celery, and cook for 10 minutes. Then add the garlic and cook for 5 minutes more. (Alternatively, this can be done in a large skillet over medium heat; cook the bacon for 10 minutes, the onion, bell pepper, and celery for 2, then the garlic for 1, and place it all in the slow cooker.)

3 Add the tomatoes, cloves, mace, allspice, clam juice, stock, potatoes, and 1 teaspoon salt to the slow cooker. Cover with the lid, reduce the setting to low, and cook for 4 hours or until the potatoes are fork-tender.

4 Add the Worcestershire, hot sauce, and ½ teaspoon salt.

5 Season the catfish pieces with salt, add them to the slow cooker, cover, and cook for 20 minutes. Add the butter to the cooker and stir it in gently. Then ladle the stew into a soup tureen or directly into individual bowls. Garnish with the parsley and banana peppers, and finish with a grind of black pepper and additional salt to taste. (Somewhere in those plates there will be 4 whole cloves. You can pick them out, or live on the edge.)

Poached Cod with Leek-Vermouth Broth

SLOW COOKER SIZE: **4+ QUARTS**
SERVES **4**
PREP TIME: **30 MINUTES**
COOK TIME: **1 HOUR AND 20 MINUTES**

Cod is a stupendously great fish when super-fresh but is like the worst fish stick when not. The cooking life becomes a lot easier and more enjoyable when you find good ingredients, so develop a relationship with a good seafood shop. (Just a platonic one.) Have that friendly fishmonger cut you beautiful thick rectangles of cod fillet, like 2½ × 2½ × 1 (those are inches). Once you get that good cod home, all you have to do is put it together with its good friend, buttery leeks.

4 (5-ounce) pieces of cod fillet

Fine sea salt

2 large leeks

¼ cup (½ stick) unsalted butter

2 cups dry vermouth

2 celery stalks, finely minced

4 bay leaves

¼ teaspoon ground Espelette chile (piment d'Espelette) or ground Korean chile (gochugaru)

Edible flowers, for garnish (optional)

1   Preheat a slow cooker on the high setting for at least 15 minutes.

2   Season the fish pieces evenly with the sea salt, as though you were sprinkling pixie dust. Arrange the fish on a wire rack set over a plate or baking dish, and place it in the refrigerator, uncovered.

3   Halve the leeks lengthwise, then rinse them carefully to remove any dirt between the layers. Pat the leeks dry, then slice them into ¼-inch-thick half-moons, discarding the root ends and the dark green parts.

4   In a large skillet set over medium-high heat, melt the butter. When it bubbles and froths, add the leeks. Cook, stirring every minute or so, for about 7 minutes, until the leeks are limp and sweet. Add the vermouth and cook for 3 minutes. Add 2 cups of water and bring to a boil. Add the celery and bay leaves, then carefully transfer the contents to the slow cooker. Cover and cook on the high setting for 1 hour.

5   Add the Espelette chile to the leek-vermouth broth and stir to incorporate it. Remove the fish from the fridge, pat it dry with paper towels, and immerse it in the broth. Cover the cooker with the lid and poach the fish on the high setting for 15 to 20 minutes, until just cooked through.

6   Serve immediately, either on a deep platter or directly onto individual plates, spooning some of the cooked leeks and cooking liquid on first, then carefully placing the fillets on top and spooning a bit more of the broth over the fish. Garnish with edible flowers, if you like.

Halibut Poached in Sherry-Pimentón Broth

SLOW COOKER SIZE: **4+ QUARTS**
SERVES **4**
PREP TIME: **25 MINUTES**
COOK TIME: **1 HOUR AND 20 MINUTES**

Halibut is a forgiving fish to poach, but I find a poach is only as good as the broth it is cooked in; this one is redolent with the flavors of Spain. The pimentón pairs beautifully with the sherry—just invest in a good dry fino sherry, not that cream sherry in your grandma's cupboard.

½ cup (1 stick) unsalted butter

4 medium shallots, small-diced

2 garlic cloves, thinly sliced

4 bay leaves

1 cup fino sherry

1 tablespoon smoked paprika

1 teaspoon ground Aleppo pepper

2 teaspoons kosher salt

1 cup Fish Stock (page 22)

4 (5-ounce) pieces of halibut

1. Turn a slow cooker to the high setting. Add the butter, and when it is melted and bubbling a bit, add the shallots, garlic, and bay leaves. Cook for 15 minutes, until the shallots and garlic have softened. Add the sherry and cook for 5 minutes; then add the paprika, Aleppo pepper, salt, and stock. Cover with the lid, turn the cooker to the low setting, and cook for 1 hour.

2. Carefully place the halibut in the stock, cover with the lid, and poach for 15 to 20 minutes, or until just cooked through. Remove the bay leaves. Serve immediately, either on a deep platter or directly onto individual plates, by spooning some of the shallots and cooking liquid first, then carefully placing the halibut on top and spooning a bit more of the broth over the fish.

Miso-Braised Salmon with Grilled Bok Choy & Sesame

SLOW COOKER SIZE: **4+ QUARTS**
SERVES **4 TO 6**
PREP TIME: **15 MINUTES**
COOK TIME: **2 HOURS AND 10 MINUTES**

Miso and fish work well together, and the mellow temperature of this poach means that you have good control over the results. It is a full-flavored dish that is appreciated by all generations (my kids always love this one). Buy wild salmon when available; you deserve that treat. It is more complex-tasting than farmed, sustainable, and supports a population of people who have been doing the hard work of fishing for centuries.

1 cup white miso paste

½ cup thinly sliced scallions (white and light green parts only from about 3 large scallions)

2 garlic cloves, thinly sliced

2 tablespoons minced fresh ginger

5 tablespoons rice vinegar

2 pounds skinless salmon fillet, cut into 4 to 6 portions

Kosher salt

Grilled Bok Choy and Sesame (recipe follows)

Sesame oil, for garnish

1   Preheat a slow cooker on the high setting for at least 15 minutes.

2   Add 3 cups of water and the miso, scallions, garlic, ginger, and vinegar to the slow cooker. Cover with the lid and cook on the high setting for 2 hours.

3   Turn the slow cooker to the low setting.

4   Season the salmon with salt. Add the salmon pieces to the slow cooker, cover with the lid, and poach for 4 minutes. Flip the salmon over, re-cover, and cook for an additional 3 to 4 minutes, until just cooked to medium rare. (If the salmon can't all fit in one layer, cook it in batches.)

5   Serve the salmon with some of the broth as a light sauce, the grilled bok choy alongside, and a drizzle of sesame oil over all.

GRILLED BOK CHOY & SESAME

SERVES 4 TO 6 AS A SIDE

12 heads baby bok choy

3 tablespoons sesame oil

Kosher salt

1½ tablespoons sesame seeds

1 Slice each bok choy head in half lengthwise. Wash the halves well, drain them on paper towels, and then pat dry. Rub the halves with the sesame oil and season each one with a sprinkle of salt.

2 Place a grill pan over high heat, or preheat a grill. When the pan is smoking, grill the bok choy for 5 minutes, flipping it over to char evenly. Transfer it to a large platter and sprinkle with the sesame seeds.

Lima Bean, Sausage & Calamari Stew with Garlic-Rubbed Toasts

SLOW COOKER SIZE: **6+ QUARTS**
SERVES **4 TO 6**
PREP TIME: **OVERNIGHT SOAK**
COOK TIME: **6 TO 8 HOURS PLUS 25 MINUTES FOR FINISHING**

I love calamari when it is cooked this way. It is a beautiful departure from the fried versions that we see around the restaurant world. The execution is very Portuguese, with the commingling of beans, sausage, and seafood—a simple dish that is sure to impress.

1 pound large dried lima beans

2 small red onions, diced

5 garlic cloves: 4 thinly sliced, 1 halved

1½ quarts Shrimp Stock (page 24) or Fish Stock (page 22)

1 cup dry red wine

3 tablespoons tomato paste

Kosher salt

1½ celery stalks, small-diced

1 pound Andouille sausage, cut into ¼-inch-thick rounds

2 teaspoons fennel seeds, toasted and ground

1 pound fresh calamari, bodies cut into 1-inch-thick rings and tentacles left whole

1 fresh baguette

2 tablespoons extra-virgin olive oil

3 tablespoons chopped fresh flat-leaf parsley leaves

1   Place the lima beans in a large bowl and add cold water to cover by at least 3 inches. Cover the bowl and soak the beans in the refrigerator overnight.

2   Drain the beans well. Add the beans, red onions, sliced garlic, stock, and red wine to a slow cooker. Cover with the lid and cook on the low setting for 5 to 7 hours, until the beans are plump and tender.

3   Add the tomato paste, 2 tablespoons salt, the celery, sausage, and fennel seeds to the slow cooker. Re-cover and cook for 1 hour.

4   Preheat the oven to 400°F.

5   Add the calamari to the slow cooker, cover with the lid, and cook for 20 minutes.

6   While the calamari is cooking, cut the baguette into diagonal ½-inch-thick slices. Drizzle the slices with the olive oil, spread them out on a baking sheet, and toast in the oven until golden brown, about 5 minutes. Remove the toasts, let them cool slightly, and then vigorously rub them with the garlic halves.

7   Stir the parsley into the stew, season with more salt if desired, and serve in individual bowls with the toasts alongside.

3 Cut the leek in half lengthwise, leaving the root end intact. Rinse the halves under cold running water to remove the dirt between the layers. Slice the halves into thin half-moons and discard the root ends and the dark green tops.

4 Add the butter, leek, garlic, bell pepper, habanero, coriander, wine, and 2 teaspoons salt to the slow cooker, cover with the lid, and cook on the low setting for 1 hour.

5 Add the lobster meat to the slow cooker, re-cover the cooker, and cook for 20 to 25 minutes, until just done. (You can uncover the cooker and hold the lobster in there for a bit while you arrange the rest of the components or wait for your guests to make their own tacos.)

6 While the lobster meat is cooking, combine the kohlrabi, mango, lime juice, tarragon, and parsley in a large bowl. When the lobster is cooked, transfer 4 tablespoons of the butter from the slow cooker to the slaw mixture, stir, and season to taste with salt.

7 Set a large cast-iron skillet over medium heat and add a touch of canola oil. When it is hot, add the tortillas, one or two at a time, and heat them through. As you process through the tortillas put them into a large sealable plastic bag to keep them warm.

8 To build a taco, spoon some of the lobster meat over 2 tortillas layered one on top of the other (or over 1 tortilla if you prefer single ply), top with the slaw and scallions, and serve with a lime wedge. And drizzle with more of the chile butter, 'cause butter and lobster are one of the happiest couples.

CHICKEN, DUCK & OTHER BIRDS . . .
plus eggs

Which came first? Ah, the eternal question. In this chapter, the Kimchi-Braised Chicken comes first, and it's so good you might actually cry, "Winner, Winner, Chicken Dinner." So get to butchering those chickens, a skill that you really should get comfortable with. Butchering a bird is rewarding in terms of cost-effectiveness, and it also gives you a bounty of neck, liver, gizzards, heart, and carcass—all champions of flavor in a from-scratch kitchen.

Simple Brine

You've heard of brining, but what does a brine actually do? It loosens the protein structure and breaks meat down to make it more tender. Some of that tenderness involves the introduction of liquid into the scenario as well, because a brined piece of meat retains some of the brine within it. Brining is always a debate, though, and it is optional in most recipes. Some fine folks (I am looking at you, Kenji López-Alt), and even yours truly on some days, believe more in dry brining by coating the protein with good sea salt (such as Maldon) and letting it rest in the fridge overnight.

All that said, liquid brines do have their place. A brine is basically a 5% to 7% salinity solution, meaning the salt, by weight, is 5% to 7% of the weight of the water and other ingredients. If you were in one of the restaurants with me, you'd be using the metric system, because the Imperial system of measurement is a system devised by a moron. Let me drop this metric bombshell on you: A liter of water is 1,000 milliliters which weighs 1 kilogram which is 1,000 grams. It is so easy being metric and so utterly confusing to be Imperial. So, I will include true metric weights here to give you a precise recipe, should you want to move on from the approximate world of the Imperial system.

This recipe makes 4 liters, or about a gallon, of brine, which, given displacement, should be enough for most brining operations. And since brine is not an expensive investment, don't worry if you have too much.

1 cup (200 grams) Diamond Crystal kosher salt

1 gallon (4 liters) cold water

4 bay leaves

1 tablespoon (20 grams) coriander seeds, toasted

6 black peppercorns

1   Combine all the ingredients in a large pot and bring to a vigorous boil over high heat. Remove the pot from the heat and let the brine cool to room temperature.

2   To use the brine, fully immerse whatever protein you are brining in the solution in a large nonreactive container. (A gallon-size heavy-duty sealable plastic bag works nicely, but make sure you set it in a large bowl in case it leaks.) Place the container in the fridge or a large cooler and let it mellow out for 24 hours.

Kimchi-Braised Chicken

SLOW COOKER SIZE: **6+ QUARTS**
SERVES **4**
PREP TIME: **25 MINUTES**
COOK TIME: **4 HOURS**

The flavors of Korea are becoming more common in the way we cook in North America. Whereas ten years ago it might have been impossible to find kimchi in a grocery store in Kansas City, now there are a couple of kinds available. This makes me happy. The umami-rich patois of the Korean pantry is so easy to include in some very basic recipes. This is a prime example of that ethos, with the simple addition of store-bought cabbage kimchi to add fiery heat and complex flavors. This is a beauty of a dish that will become a regular item in your meal cycle.

1 chicken (about 3 pounds), butchered (see page 133)

Kosher salt

1 tablespoon canola oil

2 shallots, minced

3 tablespoons minced fresh ginger

1 cup sake

1½ cups Slow Cooker Chicken Broth (page 17)

2½ cups chopped cabbage kimchi, with juices

2 tablespoons light soy sauce

Pinch of crushed red pepper flakes

2 tablespoons freshly squeezed lime juice

Rice with Mint and Cilantro (page 148)

Seasonal pickles (okra, cucumber, carrots, daikon radish), for serving

1 Pat the chicken pieces dry and season them all over with kosher salt. Place the largest skillet you have over medium heat and add the canola oil. When the oil is shimmering, place the chicken in the pan, skin-side down, and cook for 10 minutes, until the skin is crisp and much of the fat has rendered off. Flip the pieces over and cook for 3 minutes more. Transfer the chicken to a plate, and add the shallots and ginger to the skillet. Cook for 3 minutes, until softened, and then add the sake, raise the heat to high, and cook for 2 minutes.

2 Transfer the shallot mixture to a slow cooker, and then add the broth and the crisped chicken pieces; season with salt. Add 1½ cups of the chopped kimchi and the soy sauce, cover with the lid, and cook on the low setting for 4 hours.

3 Add the red pepper flakes and lime juice to the slow cooker, and stir to combine. Serve the chicken from the cooker family-style, or arrange it on individual plates, along with the rice, some pickles, and the remaining kimchi.

Chicken & Dumplings

This is a classic dish that gains deep flavor with slow cooking. Chicken and dumplings is the coq au vin of the American South: it's a dish that just makes people feel hugged, warming you up with some smart, timeless Southern goodness. It's a simple, chickeny-chicken braise, with tender, pillowy buttermilk dumplings to soak up the flavor.

6 to 8 chicken legs (about 2 pounds), brined (see page 127)

Kosher salt and freshly ground black pepper

3 tablespoons extra-virgin olive oil

1 quart Slow Cooker Chicken Broth (page 17)

1 small sweet onion, small-diced

3 celery stalks, finely diced

¼ pound oyster mushrooms, thinly sliced

2 bay leaves

1 cup all-purpose flour

¾ cup buttermilk

½ teaspoon baking powder

2 medium carrots, finely diced (1 cup)

1 tablespoon finely chopped fresh thyme leaves

2 tablespoons coarsely chopped fresh flat-leaf parsley leaves

1   Preheat a slow cooker on the low setting for 20 minutes.

2   Pat the chicken legs dry and season them well with salt and pepper.

3   Heat 2 tablespoons of the olive oil in a large skillet over medium heat. When the oil is shimmering, add the chicken legs and sear them on one side for 5 minutes. Then flip them over and sear for another 5 minutes, until nicely browned on both sides.

4   Pour the broth into the slow cooker and add the onion, half of the celery, the mushrooms, and the bay leaves. Add the chicken, cover, and cook for 4 hours.

5   Once the chicken has cooked for about 3½ hours, prepare the dumpling dough: In a medium bowl, combine the flour, buttermilk, 1 teaspoon salt, and the baking powder; mix with a fork until just combined (a few lumps are okay). When the chicken has cooked for the 4 hours, add the dumplings by dropping heaping spoonfuls (golf-ball-size) directly into the slow cooker. Cover with the lid and cook for 30 minutes; then flip the dumplings over and cook for 30 minutes more.

6   To finish the dish, place a medium skillet over medium heat and add the remaining 1 tablespoon olive oil. When the oil begins to shimmer, add the carrots, remaining celery, and a pinch of salt. Sweat the vegetables down for 3 minutes. Remove from the heat and add the thyme and parsley. Fold this mixture into the slow cooker. Serve and eat!

HOW TO BUTCHER A CHICKEN

1   Place the chicken on a clean cutting board, breast-side up. Have a clean damp towel nearby, to mop up any poultry runoff. If the innards exist, keep them if your recipe stipulates they be used, or reserve them for another use, such as simply sautéed chicken livers with shallots and Marsala over toast.

2   Thoroughly pat the chicken dry with paper towels; then, using a sharp knife, remove the legs. Pull one of the legs away from the body, and then gently slice the skin beside the thigh to expose the ball joint that connects the leg to the body of the chicken. Bend the thigh back to further expose that joint, eventually snapping it open, and then carefully cut the leg away from the carcass at the joint. (If you find the point of the joint with your knife, this should be quite easy; if you're cutting into hard bone, search a little more for the joint.) Repeat with the other leg. Then find the point at which the thigh connects to the drumstick (this is easiest if you straighten the leg as much as possible) and cut them apart. Again, this shouldn't be a very forceful cut. Repeat with the other leg. Set the 2 thighs and 2 drumsticks aside.

3   With the breast-side up, find the joints where the wings connect with the carcass. Cut the wings off and set them aside with the thighs and drumsticks.

4   Run a sharp knife down each side of the breastbone to begin to separate the breast from the rib cage. Butchery at this point is a matter of separating muscle from bone, very different from cutting through muscle. This process is done by pushing or pulling the muscle with your fingers and daintily edging it away from the bone, with small nicks and delicate nudges of the knife to help release it. Work the breast away from the wishbone, making sure that the skin is still intact. When the breast has been loosened from the breastbone, cut the last connection of skin that is holding it to the carcass. Repeat with other breast, to result in 2 boneless breasts, the meat America was built on. (You can then take each breast and cut it in half against the grain.)

5   Flip the carcass over and use a small paring knife to remove the oysters, those quarter-size lumps of meat that lie just next to the leg joints on the back of the bird. Good eatin', those oysters.

6   Save the carcass for making stock. (The recipes on pages 17 and 18 call for using whole chickens, but you can save a couple of carcasses and make a delicious stock with the same method.)

Coq au Vin

SLOW COOKER SIZE: **6+ QUARTS**
SERVES **4**
PREP TIME: **ABOUT 45 MINUTES**
COOK TIME: **3 HOURS**

I was raised in the small city of Ottawa, Canada. It is the placid capital of the country, starchy with government and stuffy with diplomacy, but it has a good, honest core to it. Across the river lies the province of Quebec, where my mind opened up to food. Quebec is the heartland of Canadian gastronomy, a place with a reverence for ingredients and technique. There are some bistros and restaurants right across the bridge from Ottawa, tucked in the Gatineau mountains, where you can learn about things as I think they would be in France (I have been to France just once—I was nine and remember only a gondola and an Alp, some white chocolate, and over-steeped tea). So Quebec, with the help of Julia Child, the only Francophile Middle America ever loved, taught me about *coq au vin*. Timeless, hearty, winey, ethereal, and a true technical braise (which means you sear the meat first, then stew it low and slow in a closed vessel), this dish shines in the slow cooker.

1 whole chicken (3 to 4 pounds)

Kosher salt and freshly ground black pepper

2 tablespoons extra-virgin olive oil

¼ pound slab bacon, small-diced

1 quart Dark Chicken Broth (page 18)

1 quart dry red wine

1 large carrot, diced

1 pound fresh cremini mushrooms:
4 mushrooms kept whole, the rest quartered

2 garlic cloves, smashed

4 bay leaves

¼ cup fresh flat-leaf parsley leaves,
coarsely chopped

1 Preheat a slow cooker on the high setting for at least 15 minutes.

2 With a pair of kitchen shears, cut the chicken in half, running the shears on either side of the breastbone, removing the breastbone and discarding, and then turning the bird over and repeating with the backbone. Season the chicken generously with salt and pepper.

3 In a large skillet set over medium heat, heat the olive oil. When the oil is shimmering, add the chicken halves, skin-side down, and sear them for 10 to 12 minutes, to brown the skin. Do this one half at a time, if necessary. Remove the chicken from the skillet and set it aside. Add the bacon to the skillet and cook it for 5 minutes, until well rendered; then add the broth and the wine and bring to a boil. Carefully pour the hot mixture into the slow cooker.

4 Add the chicken halves, carrot, quartered mushrooms, garlic, and bay leaves to the slow cooker. Cover with the lid, reduce the setting to low, and cook for 3 hours.

5 Season the coq au vin to taste with salt and pepper. Remove the bay leaves.

6 To serve, arrange the chicken halves on a platter and spoon a good bit of the braising liquid and vegetables over them. Using a mandoline, thinly slice the reserved mushrooms. Garnish the chicken with the sliced mushrooms and the parsley. I like to separate the legs into thighs and drumsticks and then carve the breast meat. Two plates get a drumstick, two plates get a thigh, and both get sliced breast.

Cider-Braised Quails with Salad of Beets, Charred Lemon, Scallions & Dates

SLOW COOKER SIZE: **6+ QUARTS**
SERVES **4**
PREP TIME: **40 MINUTES**
COOK TIME: **ABOUT 1 HOUR**

Quails are versatile little birds. If you can hunt better than Dick Cheney, you will want this recipe to help you run through the haul. If you can't, these days quails can be found, usually frozen, in a number of different styles: bone-in and all dressed up; "Euro boneless," which sounds like they would be wearing a tiny Speedo but in reality means that they are boneless except for the wing and leg bones; and even just boneless breasts and legs. This recipe can be made with any of the above, but I prefer the whole bird. Encourage your eaters to use their fingers . . . it's the way quails were meant to be eaten.

Topped with the beet salad, this becomes a modern take on a campfire classic. The beets and lemon add freshness, and the scallions and dates add sweetness.

2 small yellow onions

8 large quails, bone-in (about ⅓ pound each without giblets)

Sea salt and freshly ground black pepper

2 tablespoons unsalted butter

8 scallions (white and light green parts only)

2 tablespoons olive oil

8 Medjool dates, pitted and chopped

Bouquet garni: 1 bay leaf plus a couple of sprigs each fresh thyme and flat-leaf parsley, tied together with twine

1 (12-ounce) bottle hard apple cider

1 cup Slow Cooker Chicken Broth (page 17)

Salad of Beets, Charred Lemon, Scallions, and Dates (recipe follows)

(recipe continues)

1. Preheat a large slow cooker on the high setting for at least 15 minutes.

2. Trim the ends from the onions, then cut each into quarters and stuff an onion quarter into the body cavity of each bird. Truss each bird with some kitchen twine by simply tying the drumsticks together. Season the quails with sea salt and a pinch of black pepper, and set aside.

3. Add the butter to the slow cooker. Cut the scallions into 2-inch-long pieces and add them to the slow cooker. Cook for about 30 minutes, until they are very soft and wilted.

4. Meanwhile, in a large skillet, heat the olive oil over medium-high heat to just below smoking. In batches, gently add the quails to the oil and cook them for about 1 minute on each breast side, and then on the back for 1 more minute, until crisp all over. Transfer the quails to a paper towel–lined plate to drain.

5. Add the chopped dates, bouquet garni, and cider to the scallions in the slow cooker. Cook for 10 minutes, and then add the broth and the quails. Cover with the lid, reduce the setting to low, and cook for 1 hour.

6. Arrange the contents of the slow cooker (discarding the bouquet garni) on a deep platter and top with the Salad of Beets, Charred Lemon, Scallions, and Dates. Serve.

SALAD OF BEETS, CHARRED LEMON, SCALLIONS & DATES

SERVES 4 AS A SIDE

2 medium beets (candy-stripe beets are lovely here, but any beet will do)

8 scallions

1 tablespoon olive oil

2 lemons, sliced into $\frac{1}{8}$-inch-thick rounds

4 Medjool dates, pitted and coarsely chopped

Kosher salt and freshly ground black pepper

1 tablespoon unsalted butter

1. Peel the beets with a vegetable peeler, then thinly slice them on a mandoline; set them aside. Cut the scallions into 2-inch lengths, discarding the roots and saving the dark green tops for another use.

2. Place a large skillet (preferably cast iron) over high heat and add the olive oil. When the oil is shimmering, add the lemon slices and scallion pieces and char for 2 minutes. Reduce the heat to medium-high, add the beets and dates, and cook for 4 or 5 minutes, stirring constantly, until the beets are cooked but still have some bite to them. Remove the pan from the heat and season the contents with salt and pepper to taste. Add the butter, stirring to melt it and glaze the vegetables. Serve as a side dish or over your favorite braised meat.

Whole Chicken with Vinegar, Carrots, Shallots, Raisins & Mint

SLOW COOKER SIZE: **6+ QUARTS**
SERVES **4**
PREP TIME: **OVERNIGHT BRINE**
COOK TIME: **3 HOURS PLUS 20 MINUTES FOR FINISHING**

You need to start this dish the night before you plan to serve it, because the chicken is dry-cured with salt first, a method I learned from reading cookbooks, particularly *The Zuni Café Cookbook,* a wonderful compendium of recipes written by the dearly departed Judy Rodgers. Dry curing, due to the simple fact that salt draws out liquid, removes a lot of moisture from the skin and results in a wonderful texture once the chicken is cooked. It is a great method, and one you should try.

1 tablespoon fine sea salt

1 teaspoon sweet smoked paprika

½ teaspoon coriander seeds, toasted and ground

½ teaspoon fennel seeds, toasted and ground

1 whole chicken (3 to 4 pounds), giblets removed

8 shallots, quartered

1 cup cider vinegar

1 cup Slow Cooker Chicken Broth (page 17)

1 pound small carrots, unpeeled but washed well, greens removed and reserved

1 cup golden raisins

½ cup torn fresh mint leaves

1   In a small bowl, combine the sea salt, paprika, coriander, and fennel and mix well. Pat the chicken as dry as possible with paper towels. Liberally sprinkle the seasoning mixture over the chicken, then truss it. Place the chicken in a baking dish and chill it in the refrigerator for 8 hours or overnight.

2   Put the shallots in a slow cooker, and add the vinegar and the broth. Add the chicken to the slow cooker, breast-side up, using the shallots as a makeshift rack. Cover the cooker with the lid and cook on the high setting for 2 hours. Then add the carrots and the raisins to the cooker, re-cover it, and cook for 1 more hour.

3   When the chicken is done (it should reach 165°F at its thickest point—check it with a meat thermometer), preheat the broiler to high. Carefully transfer the chicken to a broiler-safe pan, setting it breast-side up, and broil it on the lowest rack for 10 minutes to brown the skin. Remove the chicken from the broiler and allow it to rest for 10 minutes.

4   Finely chop enough of the reserved carrot greens to make ¼ cup.

5   Place the chicken on a platter and arrange the cooked shallots, carrots, and raisins around it. Pour the remaining slow cooker juices over the chicken as a sauce. Garnish with the mint and carrot greens and serve.

Chicken Stew with Farro, Tomatoes, Olives & Feta

SLOW COOKER SIZE: **4+ QUARTS**
SERVES **4**
PREP TIME: **30 MINUTES**
COOK TIME: **4 HOURS**

Farro seems to be having a moment, and I like moments when great ingredients take the limelight. Also known as emmer wheat, farro has been a staple of the Italian kitchen for eons, but only now is it easy to find in grocery stores. It is a toothsome, nutty, super-nutritious, and easy-to-cook grain that's a great base for stews, salads, and warm grain bowls. This stew matches equally well with that fancy bottle of Burgundy or a nice cold PBR. Your choice.

4 skin-on, bone-in chicken thighs

Kosher salt and freshly ground black pepper

2 tablespoons extra-virgin olive oil

1 large sweet onion, large-diced

2 medium carrots, small-diced

1½ cups farro

4 sprigs fresh rosemary

2 quarts Slow Cooker Chicken Broth (page 17)

1 pound heirloom tomatoes, coarsely chopped

1 cup Kalamata olives, pitted but left whole

1 cup crumbled feta cheese

2 tablespoons coarsely chopped fresh marjoram leaves

1   Preheat a slow cooker on the low setting for at least 20 minutes.

2   Pat the chicken thighs dry and season them with salt and pepper. Place a large skillet over medium heat and add the olive oil. When the oil begins to shimmer, add the chicken thighs, skin-side down, and cook for 10 minutes, until well-browned. Then flip them over and cook for 3 minutes more. Transfer the chicken to a plate.

3   Add the onion and carrots to the skillet and cook over medium heat, scraping up some of the browned bits, for 3 minutes, until starting to soften. Add the farro and rosemary sprigs and cook for 3 minutes, to toast the farro. Transfer this mixture to the slow cooker, place the chicken thighs on top of the farro, and then add the broth and salt to taste. Cover with the lid and cook on the low setting for 4 hours.

4   Divide the chicken among individual bowls. Add the tomatoes, olives, ¾ cup of the feta, and 1 tablespoon of the marjoram to the slow cooker and stir to warm them. Season to taste with salt and pepper. Stir again, pull out the rosemary sprigs, and then ladle the mixture over the chicken. Garnish with the remaining marjoram and feta.

Chicken Country Captain

SLOW COOKER SIZE: **4+ QUARTS**
SERVES **4**
PREP TIME: **35 MINUTES**
COOK TIME: **4 HOURS**

Country Captain is a complex dish that travels the spice route of Southern history, featuring bright flavors that were introduced through the ports of Savannah and Charleston centuries ago. It is Indian-inspired through the lens of the West Indies, with a heavy dose of West Africa. The almonds and raisins provide textural finish, the chile is mellowed with the coconut milk, and the rich chicken shines with the garlic and ginger. So yes, it is complex but when I say complex, I mean in flavor—this is not a difficult dish to make, and the results will please a whole brood of people.

2 tablespoons unsalted butter

4 skin-on, bone-in chicken legs

Kosher salt

1 medium sweet onion, medium-diced

1 poblano chile, seeded and finely diced

2 garlic cloves, minced

1 (1-inch) piece fresh ginger, cut into matchsticks

1 tablespoon curry powder

1 pound fresh tomatoes, diced

2 bay leaves

1 quart Slow Cooker Chicken Broth (page 17)

1 cup coconut milk

¼ cup golden raisins

¼ cup sliced blanched almonds

2 scallions (white and light green parts), sliced

1 quart Rice with Mint and Cilantro (recipe follows) or plain cooked long-grain rice

1   Preheat a slow cooker on the high setting for at least 15 minutes.

2   Melt the butter in a large sauté pan over medium heat.

3   Put the chicken legs on a cutting board, and using a sharp knife, cut through the joint separating the thighs and drumsticks. Pat the pieces dry and season them with salt. Place the pieces, skin-side down, in the pan and crisp the skin for 10 to 15 minutes. Remove from the pan and set it aside.

4   Add the onion to the pan and cook, scraping up the browned chicken bits, for 3 minutes, until translucent. Add the poblano, garlic, and ginger and cook for 2 minutes. Add the curry, tomatoes, bay leaves, broth, and 1 teaspoon salt. Bring to a boil, then transfer the mixture to the slow cooker.

5   Add the chicken pieces, skin-side up, to the slow cooker and cover with the lid. Reduce the setting to low and cook for 4 hours.

6   Remove the chicken pieces and arrange them on a platter. Add the coconut milk, raisins, and almonds to the braising liquid and stir to combine. Spoon the sauce over the chicken, garnish with the scallions, and serve with the rice.

2 cups long-grain rice, such as jasmine

⅓ cup chopped fresh mint leaves

⅓ cup chopped fresh cilantro leaves and stems

Kosher salt

1   Place the rice and 4 cups of cool water in a
    slow cooker. Cover with the lid and cook for
    2 hours on the low setting.

2   Turn off the heat, fluff the rice with a fork,
    add the mint and cilantro, and season to
    taste with salt.

Duck Legs Cacciatore

SLOW COOKER SIZE: **4+ QUARTS**
SERVES **4**
PREP TIME: **35 MINUTES**
COOK TIME: **5 HOURS**

Cacciatore has come to mean "hunter's style," though the term really just refers to the hunter. Nevertheless, I get it. It is a dish that you could cook in the woods, but with a slow cooker you'd need a long extension cord. It is an easy braise made savory with olives, bell peppers, capers, and anchovies. I would serve this with bread or over soft polenta (which you can cook just like grits, page 51) and a simple green salad on the side.

4 duck legs, visible fat trimmed and saved for another use

Kosher salt

2 tablespoons all-purpose flour

1 cup extra-virgin olive oil

1 large sweet onion, sliced into ¼-inch-thick rounds

1 large red bell pepper, seeded and sliced

6 garlic cloves, thinly sliced

1 cup pitted Gaeta or Kalamata olives

¼ cup capers

1 tablespoon chopped canned anchovies

1 (28-ounce) can San Marzano tomatoes

1 cup Slow Cooker Chicken Broth (page 17)

Freshly ground black pepper

¼ cup chopped fresh flat-leaf parsley leaves

12 fresh sage leaves

2 button mushrooms, for garnish

1 Preheat a slow cooker on the high setting.

2 Meanwhile, place the duck legs on a cutting board, and using a sharp boning knife, separate each thigh from the drumstick by cutting through the joint. Season the duck pieces with salt, and then sprinkle them with the flour to lightly coat. (I am not a big fan of a ton of flour in a recipe like this: a little bit goes a long way in binding everything together.)

3 Place a large skillet over medium heat and add ¼ cup of the olive oil. When the oil is shimmering, add the duck pieces, skin-side down. Let them crisp slowly, for about 15 minutes, and then turn them over and crisp for 10 minutes on the other side.

(recipe continues)

4 While the duck is crisping, take a couple of tablespoons of the fat out of the duck pan and pour it into the slow cooker. Add the onion, bell pepper, and garlic to the cooker, cover with the lid, and cook, stirring once in a while, for 20 minutes, until softened. Add the olives, capers, anchovies, and tomatoes and cook for 10 minutes. (Alternatively, you can do this in a large sauté pan, cooking the onion, pepper, and garlic for 10 minutes and the olives and the rest for 5 minutes more before adding the broth.) Transfer the mixture to the slow cooker. Then pour the broth in as well. Add the seared duck, season it with about 1 teaspoon salt (or to taste), and reduce the slow cooker setting to low. Stir, cover with the lid, and cook for 5 hours.

5 Season the duck with salt and pepper to taste, and stir in the parsley.

6 For garnish, let's fry some sage: Pour the remaining ¾ cup olive oil into a small pot and warm it over medium-high heat. Place a paper towel–lined plate next to the stovetop and keep a slotted spoon handy. When the oil is hot (around 325°F—measure it with a deep-frying or candy thermometer), add the sage leaves and cook until crisp, 10 to 20 seconds. Remove them with the slotted spoon and let them drain on the paper towels. Remove the pot from the heat and let the olive oil cool, but don't throw it out. Instead, save it for another use, like drizzling it over that butternut squash soup you're gonna cook next week.

7 Arrange the duck on a large, deep platter, spoon the braising sauce over it, and garnish with the fried sage leaves. Using a mandoline, shave the button mushrooms very thinly and scatter them over everything.

Duck Confit with Simple Frisée Salad

SLOW COOKER SIZE: 6+ QUARTS

SERVES 4

PREP TIME: OVERNIGHT BRINE PLUS 30 MINUTES

COOK TIME: 8 TO 12 HOURS

Duck confit is just one of those things that give an inordinate amount of culinary satisfaction. Done right, the meat is silky and tender, and crisped on the outside. Doing it right with duck confit means simmering the duck very gently in fat; too hot and it fries, making it stringy and dry. Not good. But that's where the slow cooker comes in—its mellow heat almost guarantees success.

Historically (before the age of modern appliances), the purpose of curing, then slow-cooking and immersing something in fat, was to keep that something from spoiling. If you re-create the same process in your slow cooker, keep the confit totally covered in fat, then stick it in that magic box of modern convenience called the fridge, it will keep for several weeks (and up to six months if the container you're keeping it in is spotlessly clean and you don't dig in there with grubby fingers).

½ cup kosher salt

2 tablespoons sugar

1 tablespoon coriander seeds, toasted and ground

2 tablespoons freshly ground black pepper

Grated zest of 1 orange

Grated zest of 1 lemon

4 skin-on, bone-in duck legs

5 cups canola oil, or more as needed

6 sprigs fresh thyme

4 garlic cloves, smashed

Simple Frisée Salad (recipe follows)

1   In a large mixing bowl, combine the salt, sugar, coriander, 1 tablespoon of the pepper, and all the citrus zest. Place the duck legs on a platter, in a large plastic container, or on a rimmed baking sheet, and liberally sprinkle the salt cure over each leg, covering it well. Cover with a lid or plastic wrap, and let cure in the refrigerator for at least 12 hours, but no more than 24 hours.

(recipe continues)

2   Combine the canola oil, thyme sprigs, garlic, and remaining 1 tablespoon black pepper in a 6-quart or larger slow cooker, turn it to the high setting, and warm the ingredients for 20 minutes. Remove the duck legs from the cure, brushing off any excess with a pastry brush. Rinse the legs lightly under cold water and pat dry. Put the legs in the slow cooker, making sure they are completely immersed in the oil, then cover the cooker with the lid. Reduce the setting to low and cook for 8 to 12 hours, until the skin on the end of the drumsticks starts to peel back and the duck is very tender when pierced with a knife. (At this point you can transfer the duck legs to a container, cover them completely with the fat, and let them cool; then store in the fridge.)

3   To serve, carefully remove the duck legs from the fat and set them on a paper towel–lined plate to drain. Place a large skillet over medium-high heat and add 2 tablespoons of the confit oil from the slow cooker. When the oil begins to shimmer, place the duck legs in the skillet, skin-side down, and cook for about 3 minutes to crisp them, then turn them over and cook for 2 more minutes to heat through. (If you are crisping after refrigerating them, flip them every few minutes, lower the heat to medium-low, and cook until heated through.)

4   Place the crisped duck legs on individual plates and garnish with the Simple Frisée Salad. Serve.

SIMPLE FRISÉE SALAD

SERVES 4 AS A SIDE OR GARNISH

2 tablespoons crème fraîche

½ tablespoon freshly squeezed lemon juice

½ teaspoon sugar

Kosher salt

2 heads frisée (curly endive), rinsed well, dark green tips removed

2 tablespoons chopped fresh chives

2 tablespoons chopped fresh tarragon leaves

In a medium bowl, whisk the crème fraîche, lemon juice, sugar, and a pinch of salt together. Tear or chop the frisée and add it to the bowl. Add the chives and tarragon, and toss well. Serve immediately.

Poached Eggs in Romesco with Potato Crisps

SLOW COOKER SIZE: **6+ QUARTS**
SERVES **4 TO 8**
PREP TIME: **25 MINUTES**
COOK TIME: **40 MINUTES, THEN 30 MINUTES**

This dish is a no-brainer for a simple brunch. Romesco is a full-flavored beauty of a sauce, thickened with nuts and redolent with smoked paprika. The romesco cooks for a while and then the eggs are nestled in it. Thirty minutes later, you have a beautiful meal, with some crisps alongside for nibbling. This is also great served over grits (page 51).

2 large red bell peppers, seeded and large-diced

2 large red tomatoes, large-diced

2 shallots, large-diced

2 garlic cloves, smashed

1 slice bread (whatever you have), cut into ½-inch pieces (about ¾ cup)

¼ cup whole skinned hazelnuts

1 cup extra-virgin olive oil

Kosher salt

1 teaspoon freshly ground black pepper

½ teaspoon crushed red pepper flakes

1½ tablespoons sweet smoked paprika

3 tablespoons sherry vinegar

8 large eggs

¼ cup chopped fresh flat-leaf parsley leaves

Potato Crisps (recipe follows) or a large bag of your favorite potato chips

Crusty bread, sliced, for serving

1   Preheat a slow cooker on the high setting for at least 15 minutes, and preheat the oven to 425°F.

2   On a rimmed baking sheet, toss the bell peppers, tomatoes, shallots, garlic, bread pieces, and hazelnuts with 2 tablespoons of the olive oil, 1 teaspoon salt, and the black pepper. Toast in the oven for 15 minutes, or until the mixture has softened and browned a bit.

3   Carefully transfer the mixture to a blender and add the remaining olive oil, the red pepper flakes, paprika, and vinegar. Blend until smooth.

4   Add the puree to the preheated slow cooker. Pour in 1½ cups of water, stir to combine, cover with the lid, and cook on the high setting for 30 minutes. Then reduce the setting to low and cook for another 10 minutes.

(recipe continues)

5 Uncover the cooker and season the sauce to taste with salt. Crack the eggs, one by one, into the romesco sauce in the cooker, holding the eggs very close to the sauce so that they nestle into it rather than spreading out. Be careful, lest you burn your fingers! Try to fit in as many eggs as you can without overcrowding the cooker. My large one fit 8 eggs comfortably. Cover the cooker with the lid and cook on the low setting for exactly 30 minutes (so as not to overcook the eggs).

6 Serve the eggs and romesco immediately, sprinkled with the chopped parsley and some of the potato chips—and bread and more chips on the side for brunch-time snacking.

POTATO CRISPS

MAKES 2 QUARTS

½ pound fingerling potatoes

2 cups canola oil

Sea salt

1 Using a mandoline, slice the potatoes paper-thin. (Use the safety guard when using a mandoline unless you just think your fingers are too long.) Immerse the potato slices in a bowl of cold water for 20 minutes to rid them of some of their starch; then dry them very well. You may want to use a hair dryer on low. For real. You want them really dry so that when you fry them, the oil doesn't spit out at you (oil and water no amigos).

2 Heat the canola oil in a large pot over medium-high heat to reach and maintain a temperature of 300°F (check it with a deep-frying or candy thermometer). In batches (so as not to overcrowd the pot or lower the temperature of the oil), add the potato slices to the hot oil and cook for 5 minutes, stirring frequently, or until golden brown and crispy. With a slotted spoon, transfer the crisp potatoes to a paper towel–lined plate to drain. Season each batch immediately with a pinch of sea salt.

HERE'S THE BEEF

Braising is a wonderful way to show off many lesser-known or underappreciated cuts of meat, which are now more widely available than ever. These cuts may not be as immediately tender as a rib eye, but what they lack in grillability they give back tenfold in flavor and texture when simmered slowly to melt all their connective tissue. From cheeks to chuck, tongue to shanks, the slow cooker is your bovine cookery companion. So get thee to the butcher and ask for those odd cuts.

Pörkölt (a.k.a. Goulash, a.k.a. Hungarian Beef)

SLOW COOKER SIZE: **6+ QUARTS**
SERVES **6 TO 8**
PREP TIME: **40 MINUTES**
COOK TIME: **4 HOURS**

Pörkölt has no pork in it, just as hamburgers have no ham. I remember the first time I made goulash and being flabbergasted at how easy it was to create something so pleasing, so aromatic, and so warming to the soul. It's a classic red wine–tomato braised beef, but full of paprika and the surprise of caraway. Goulash is déjà vu for me. I don't know why or where I enjoyed it in my youth, but I have some emotional attachment to it. Apart from being secretly Canadian, maybe I am secretly Hungarian as well.

3 pounds boneless beef shoulder, cut into 1-inch cubes

Kosher salt

4 tablespoons vegetable oil

2 large onions, diced

6 garlic cloves, shaved or very thinly sliced

1 teaspoon caraway seeds

1 cup dry red wine

3 cups Beef Shin Stock (page 21)

¼ cup sweet Hungarian paprika

4 yellow Hungarian wax, Cubanelle, or Anaheim chiles, seeded and sliced

1 (28-ounce) can plum tomatoes with juices

1 cup shaved or very thinly sliced parsnip

3 scallions (white and light green parts only), chopped

Garnishes: sour cream, pickles, paprika, dill, and crusty bread

1 Preheat a slow cooker on the high setting for at least 15 minutes.

2 Season the beef all over with salt.

3 Place the largest skillet you have over medium-high heat and add 2 tablespoons of the vegetable oil. When the oil shimmers, add half of the beef in an even layer and brown for about 2 minutes per side, until evenly browned, a total of 6 to 8 minutes. Transfer the beef to a large baking sheet. Repeat with the remaining oil and beef. Add the onions to the skillet and cook for 15 minutes, stirring, until golden. Add the garlic and the caraway, return the beef to the skillet, and add the red wine. Cook until the wine has reduced by half, about 3 minutes. Then add the stock, paprika, chiles, 1½ teaspoons salt, and the tomatoes.

4 Transfer the contents of the skillet to the slow cooker, cover, and cook on the high setting for 4 hours, until the beef is very tender. Taste, and add more salt if necessary.

5 Serve with a scattering of parsnips and scallions, sour cream, some chopped pickles of your choice, paprika, a few dill fronds, and crusty bread for mopping up the juices.

Beef Cheeks with Parsnip Puree & Apple Slaw

SLOW COOKER SIZE: **4+ QUARTS**
SERVES **4**
PREP TIME: **15 MINUTES**
COOK TIME: **4 HOURS**

Cheeks are made for braising due to the fact that animals chew, which produces a hardworking muscle. Muscles that work hard develop a ton of flavor and are dense, with good marbling and connective tissue that becomes meltingly tender when braised. You don't have to be married to beef cheeks: veal, pork, or even lamb cheeks work well, though lambs have little cheeks. Braise on, my friends.

2 pounds beef cheeks, trimmed of excess fat and sinew

Kosher salt

1 teaspoon freshly ground black pepper

1 tablespoon olive oil

1 quart Beef Shin Stock (page 21)

1 quart dry red wine

1 large onion, large-diced

2 medium carrots, large-diced

3 celery stalks, large-diced

4 sprigs fresh rosemary

2 sprigs fresh thyme

1 bay leaf

1 teaspoon allspice berries

1 cup Parsnip Puree (recipe follows)

Apple Slaw (recipe follows), for garnish

1   Preheat a slow cooker on the high setting for at least 15 minutes.

2   Pat the beef cheeks dry and season them all over with salt and the black pepper.

3   Set a large braising pan, such as a Dutch oven, over high heat and add the olive oil. When the oil begins to shimmer, add the beef cheeks and sear them for about 3 minutes per side, until golden brown. Transfer the cheeks to a plate to rest. Add the stock and red wine to the braising pan and bring to a boil, scraping up any browned bits. Add the onion, carrots, and celery and bring back to a boil. Remove the pan from the heat and carefully pour the contents into the slow cooker.

4   Add the seared beef cheeks, rosemary and thyme sprigs, bay leaf, and allspice berries to the slow cooker. Cover with the lid, reduce the setting to low, and cook for 4 hours. Remove the rosemary and thyme sprigs.

5   To serve, place a dollop of Parsnip Puree on each dinner plate, arrange the cheeks over the puree, and drizzle with some of the braising liquid. Garnish each serving with Apple Slaw.

PARSNIP PUREE

You can substitute this dish in many recipes that call for mashed potatoes; the puree is an excellent side for any braised meat. It will keep in the refrigerator for up to a week.

SERVES 4 TO 8 AS A SIDE

2 tablespoons unsalted butter

2 shallots, thinly sliced

2 garlic cloves, thinly sliced

Kosher salt

1 pound parsnips, halved lengthwise and sliced into ¼-inch-thick half-moons

1 cup heavy cream

3 tablespoons freshly squeezed lemon juice

In a medium pot set over medium heat, melt the butter. When the butter bubbles and froths, add the shallots, garlic, and 1 teaspoon salt and cook for 3 minutes. Add the parsnips, stir well, and cook for another 3 minutes. Add 1 cup of water and the heavy cream, and simmer for about 15 minutes, until the parsnips are soft. Carefully transfer the mixture to a blender, add the lemon juice, and puree until smooth. Season with salt to taste.

APPLE SLAW

SERVES 4 AS A SIDE

2 teaspoons grated lemon zest

2 teaspoons freshly squeezed lemon juice

2 tablespoons crème fraîche

¼ teaspoon kosher salt, plus more if needed

½ teaspoon sugar

2 green apples, cored and julienned

4 scallions (white and light green parts), thinly sliced

1 tablespoon celery seeds

In a large bowl, combine the lemon zest, lemon juice, crème fraîche, salt, and sugar. Whisk to blend, and then toss with the apples, scallions, and celery seeds. Season with additional salt if desired.

Pot Roast with Charred Onion & Chickpea Salad

SLOW COOKER SIZE: **6+ QUARTS**
SERVES **6 TO 8**
PREP TIME: **25 MINUTES**
COOK TIME: **8 TO 10 HOURS**

This is a perfect early fall meal, capturing the abundance of peppers and onions that the harvest has brought. Pot roast sometimes gets a bad rap for being dry, boring, and bland. I understand the hesitation with dishes that maybe you had bad versions of growing up, but this recipe shines a new light on a classic. Using chuck and cooking it slow-and-low allows it time to fully develop its flavor. Pair it with a fresh chickpea salad to brighten up the dish.

1 boneless beef chuck roast (about 3 pounds)

Kosher salt

1 tablespoon freshly ground black pepper

2 tablespoons canola oil

4 medium carrots, large-diced

1 large sweet onion, large-diced

6 garlic cloves, smashed

6 bay leaves

6 sprigs fresh thyme

1 quart Beef Shin Stock (page 21)

1 quart dry red wine

1 tablespoon coriander seeds, toasted and ground

Charred Onion and Chickpea Salad (recipe follows)

1   Pat the chuck roast dry and season it all over with salt and the pepper.

2   Place a large braising pan, such as a Dutch oven, over high heat and warm the canola oil in it until it shimmers. Add the chuck roast and sear it for about 5 minutes per side, until nicely browned. Transfer the roast to a plate to rest, and add the carrots and onion to the braising pan. Cook for 3 minutes on high heat, stirring, until the vegetables are starting to soften; then add the garlic, bay leaves, and thyme sprigs and cook for 1 minute more. Add the stock, red wine, and ground coriander and deglaze the pan, scraping up any browned bits. Cook for 5 minutes.

3   Remove the pan from the heat and carefully pour the contents into a slow cooker. Add the chuck roast, cover with the lid, and cook on the low setting for 8 to 10 hours, until very tender. Season with additional salt, if desired.

4   Transfer the roast to a platter, discard the bay and thyme, and serve the Charred Onion and Chickpea Salad alongside.

CHARRED ONION &
CHICKPEA SALAD

SERVES 6 TO 8 AS A SIDE

1 tablespoon canola oil

1 large red onion, halved lengthwise, root end of each half left intact

2 (15-ounce) cans chickpeas, drained and rinsed, or 10 ounces dried chickpeas, cooked (see page 97)

2 cups coarsely chopped fresh cilantro (from about 1 bunch)

4 red jalapeño peppers, thinly sliced

3 tablespoons freshly squeezed lemon juice

2 tablespoons extra-virgin olive oil

1 tablespoon ground cumin

Kosher salt

1 Heat a small skillet over medium-high heat. Add the canola oil, and when it begins to shimmer, add the onion halves, cut-side down, and char for about 10 minutes—you want them to be well blackened. Remove the skillet from the heat and let the onion halves cool to room temperature; then slice each half into ¼-inch-thick half-rings.

2 In a medium bowl, combine the chickpeas, cilantro, jalapeños, charred onion slices, lemon juice, olive oil, and cumin. Toss well and season with salt to taste.

Corned Beef Brisket with Cabbage, Potatoes & Dill

SLOW COOKER SIZE: **6+ QUARTS**
SERVES **6**
PREP TIME: **1 WEEK CURE PLUS 35 MINUTES**
COOK TIME: **8 TO 10 HOURS**

This recipe requires that you start seven days ahead of time to brine the brisket, but I promise, it's worth it. Corned beef is timeless and deserves a spot at the table, not just on St. Paddy's Day. It is a crowd-pleaser that loves the low-and-slow ethos of the slow cooker, turning it tender without fail.

Instacure is a nitrate that is optional to the recipe, but recommended because you are brining the beef for a long time and it will ensure that nothing goes wrong, microbe-wise. It will also make the meat retain its characteristic pinkish color. You can purchase Instacure online.

2 cups apple juice

2 tablespoons real maple syrup

1 teaspoon Instacure #1 (optional)

1 teaspoon yellow mustard seeds

½ teaspoon Tellicherry black peppercorns

1 teaspoon caraway seeds

½ teaspoon allspice berries

4 bay leaves

Kosher salt

1 quart ice cubes

4 pounds beef brisket (fatty or lean, up to you)

1 tablespoon olive oil

2 medium yellow onions, halved

2 tablespoons brown miso paste

4 garlic cloves

2 tablespoons unsalted butter

1 head Savoy cabbage, sliced into thin ribbons (about 3 cups)

Dill Potatoes (recipe follows)

2 tablespoons chopped fresh dill

¼ cup Pickled Mustard Seeds (page 183)

1   Pour 1½ quarts of cold water and the apple juice into a large pot and bring to a boil. Add the maple syrup, Instacure, mustard seeds, peppercorns, ½ teaspoon of the caraway seeds, the allspice berries, bay leaves, and ½ cup salt. Cook for 3 minutes at a rapid boil; then remove from the heat. Add the ice and wait for the brine to cool to room temperature.

2   Place the brisket in a large container and cover it fully with the brine. (If you have an extra-large sealable plastic bag, those work really well, keeping the meat fully immersed in the brine.) Cover with a lid or plastic wrap and store in the refrigerator for 1 week.

3   After that week, remove the brisket from the brine and strain the brine, saving the spices and bay leaves and discarding the liquid. Set the brisket aside on a plate.

4   Preheat a large slow cooker on the low setting for at least 20 minutes.

5   In large skillet, warm the olive oil over medium-high heat. When the oil begins

to shimmer, add the onions and cook for 15 minutes, turning them once in a while, until they are well browned and a touch charred.

6 Place the brisket in the slow cooker and add the charred onions, miso, garlic, 1 tablespoon of the butter, and the strained spices and bay leaves. Add enough room-temperature water to cover the brisket by 2 inches. Cover with the lid and cook on the low setting for 8 to 10 hours, until the brisket is really tender—a paring knife should plunge into the meat with little resistance. Skim off any fat that has risen to the surface.

7 Place a large skillet over medium-high heat and add the remaining 1 tablespoon butter. When it begins to bubble and froth, add the cabbage, remaining ½ teaspoon caraway seeds, and ½ teaspoon salt. Stir to combine; then let the cabbage char for 2 minutes to develop some color. Toss the cabbage and cook for another 2 minutes. Then transfer it to a large platter.

8 Remove the brisket from the slow cooker, taking care to keep it in one piece. Place it on top of the cabbage on the platter, let it rest for 5 minutes, and then slice it into ½-inch-thick slabs, against the grain. It will be very tender, and it may fall apart. That's okay. We want that. Add the potatoes to the platter. Garnish with the fresh dill and the Pickled Mustard Seeds.

DILL POTATOES

SERVES 6 AS A SIDE

1 pound fingerling potatoes

Kosher salt

1 tablespoon unsalted butter

1 tablespoon finely chopped fresh dill

Place the fingerling potatoes in a medium pot, add cool water to cover by 1 inch, and bring to a boil over high heat. Add salt to taste, reduce the heat, and simmer for 10 to 15 minutes, until the potatoes are fork-tender. Remove the pot from the heat and drain off the water. Toss the potatoes well with the butter and the chopped dill, melting the butter. Season with additional salt to taste, and serve.

Veal Meatballs, Swiss Chard & Tomato Sauce

SLOW COOKER SIZE: **4+ QUARTS**
SERVES **4 TO 6**
PREP TIME: **35 MINUTES**
COOK TIME: **2 HOURS**

Meatballs are something I can serve to three generations of my family and know everybody will be happy. That kind of dish is a keeper! These meatballs are classic, lightened with ricotta cheese, insanely easy, and will feed four very hungry people with ease. If you prefer to make them with ground lamb or beef instead, go right ahead.

2 pounds ground veal

1 cup ricotta cheese

2 large eggs, beaten

1 cup dried bread crumbs

1½ tablespoons finely chopped fresh thyme leaves

Kosher salt and freshly ground black pepper

2 tablespoons canola oil

1 small onion, large-diced

4 garlic cloves, thinly sliced

½ cup white balsamic vinegar

1 (32-ounce) can San Marzano tomatoes

¼ cup fresh basil leaves, torn, plus more for garnish

1 large bunch Swiss chard, stems minced and leaves cut into bite-size pieces

½ cup grated Parmigiano-Reggiano cheese

1   In a large bowl, combine the veal, ricotta, eggs, bread crumbs, thyme, 1 tablespoon salt, and 1 teaspoon pepper. Mix well with your hands, and then form the mixture into about sixteen 3-ounce meatballs (1½ to 2 inches in diameter).

2   In a large skillet, heat the canola oil over medium-high heat. When the oil is shimmering, add the meatballs, in batches if necessary, and sear them for about 8 minutes, until golden brown on several sides. Remove the meatballs and set them aside. Add the onion and garlic to the skillet and cook for 3 minutes, until translucent. Add the balsamic vinegar and cook for 3 minutes, until the skillet is nearly dry. Then add the tomatoes and their liquid, and cook for another 3 minutes. Scrape the tomato mixture into a blender or food processor, add the basil, and pulse until a coarse tomato sauce is formed. Pour the sauce into a slow cooker, nestle the meatballs into the sauce, cover with the lid, and cook on the high setting for 2 hours.

3   Remove the meatballs and add the Swiss chard to the tomato sauce, stirring well to wilt it. Season the sauce with salt and pepper to taste.

4   Ladle some of the sauce, with the Swiss chard, into individual shallow bowls, and divide the meatballs among the bowls. Drizzle with a bit more sauce and garnish with a healthy sprinkle of Parmigiano-Reggiano and torn basil leaves.

Pancetta-Mushroom Beef Rolls with Tomato Salad

SLOW COOKER SIZE: **4+ QUARTS**
SERVES **4 TO 6**
PREP TIME: **30 MINUTES**
COOK TIME: **40 MINUTES**

It's *braciole* or *involtini* . . . same thing, pretty much. Regardless of the name, it is delicious. And easy. Beautiful flat iron steak is butterflied and stuffed with flavors we love—pancetta, mushrooms, spinach, and cheese. It is tied up with care and braised lusciously. And it is an inexpensive treat of a meal. So get stuffing 'cause this recipe is a winner.

2 pounds flat iron steak, butterflied into a large, flat rectangle

Kosher salt and freshly ground black pepper

1 tablespoon extra-virgin olive oil, plus more for searing

6 ounces pancetta, small-diced (1 cup)

1 medium onion, small-diced

4 garlic cloves, thinly sliced

½ pound fresh cremini mushrooms, thinly sliced

½ pound fresh spinach

¼ cup grated Parmigiano-Reggiano cheese

2 cups Beef Shin Stock (page 21)

2 tablespoons tomato paste

4 sprigs fresh rosemary

Tomato Salad (recipe follows)

1 Preheat a slow cooker on the low setting for at least 20 minutes.

2 Lay out the beef and season it all over with salt and 1 tablespoon pepper.

3 Heat the olive oil in a sauté pan over medium heat. Add the pancetta and cook for 5 minutes, until it begins to brown and render some of the fat. Add the onion, garlic, and mushrooms and cook for 5 minutes. Add the spinach, and season with more salt and pepper, to taste. Remove the pan from the heat, but keep everything in the pan for 3 minutes, stirring until the spinach is fully wilted. Strain off any liquid, then add the cheese to the spinach mixture; stir to combine, and set aside to cool.

4 When the spinach mixture is cool, scoop it onto the center of the beef slab and smooth it out, as if you were icing a cake. Roll the beef tightly around the stuffing (see photographs opposite) and tie off each end with butcher's twine.

(recipe continues)

5 Heat a large, heavy skillet over high heat. Coat the pan with olive oil and pat the beef dry. When the oil comes to a light smoke, sear the beef for 2 to 3 minutes per side, until browned.

6 Pour the stock into the slow cooker, and add the tomato paste and rosemary sprigs. Stir to dissolve the tomato paste. Then add the beef roll, cover with the lid, and cook on the low setting for 40 minutes.

7 Remove the beef roll from the slow cooker and let it rest for 5 to 10 minutes prior to slicing. Slice it into 1-inch-thick medallions, and serve with the Tomato Salad alongside.

TOMATO SALAD

This is a simple salad that would be a great accompaniment to many slow cooker recipes, such as Chicken and Dumplings (page 131) or Goat and Garlic (page 229). It will balance any rich braised meat.

SERVES 4 TO 6 AS A SIDE

¼ cup good-quality extra-virgin olive oil

1 tablespoon red wine vinegar

1 tablespoon freshly squeezed lemon juice

1 English cucumber, peeled, seeded, and finely diced (optional)

1 pound heirloom tomatoes, diced

1 large shallot, minced

½ cup chopped fresh flat-leaf parsley leaves

Kosher salt and freshly ground black pepper

4 cups seasonal greens, such as arugula, purslane, spinach, or kale, torn into bite-size pieces

1 Combine the olive oil, vinegar, and lemon juice in a small Mason jar, screw on the top, and shake to combine.

2 In a large nonreactive bowl, combine the cucumber, tomatoes, shallot, and parsley. Add the vinaigrette and toss. Season with salt and pepper to taste. Let the mixture sit at room temperature for 1 hour. Just prior to serving, toss in the greens.

Mustard-Braised Beef Tongue

SLOW COOKER SIZE: **4+ QUARTS**

SERVES **4 TO 6**

PREP TIME: **15 MINUTES**

COOK TIME: **8 HOURS**

You can eat this dish any way you please, but I recommend serving it thinly sliced on a piece of buttered toasted rye bread, schmeared with pickled mustard seeds and topped with caramelized onions. The meaty, deep, rich flavor of tongue is like steak crossed with a little bit of liver, and to me, it's one of the best cuts of meat there is. Don't tell the kids they are eating tongue, and I promise they'll love it, too.

1 tablespoon extra-virgin olive oil

1 small sweet onion, large-diced

1 garlic clove, thinly sliced

1 quart Beef Shin Stock (page 21)

¼ cup whole-grain mustard

4 pounds beef tongue, brined overnight (see page 127)

6 bay leaves

Kosher salt

2 teaspoons freshly ground black pepper

1 teaspoon freshly ground caraway seeds

Pickled Mustard Seeds (recipe follows)

1 Set a slow cooker on the high setting, add the olive oil, and heat it until it begins to shimmer. Then add the onion and garlic and cook for 10 minutes, until softened. Add the stock and the mustard, and cook for 5 minutes.

2 Add the beef tongue, bay leaves, salt, pepper, and caraway to the slow cooker. Cover with the lid, reduce the setting to low, and cook for 8 hours.

3 Once it is tender, remove the tongue from the slow cooker and let it cool until it is comfortable to handle. Carefully remove the tough exterior membrane by simply peeling it off with your hands. Return the tongue to the braising mixture and leave it there until you are ready to eat. Before serving, thinly slice the beef tongue against the grain. Serve it up with some Pickled Mustard Seeds.

PICKLED MUSTARD SEEDS

Mustard seeds that have been plumped in a pickle brine can really make a dish. They provide texture and crunch, heat and sweetness. And as a bonus, they will stay fresh in the fridge for about a month. Sprinkle them over everything, from a nice braised pork butt to a simple salad, for added brightness.

MAKES ABOUT 1 CUP IN BRINE

½ cup yellow mustard seeds

1 cup champagne vinegar

1 tablespoon sugar

1 teaspoon kosher salt

1   Place the mustard seeds in a small pot, cover with cold water, and bring the liquid to a boil. Strain the mustard seeds, discarding the water, and repeat this process 3 more times.

2   In the same pot, combine 1 cup of cold water with the vinegar, sugar, salt, and the blanched mustard seeds. Bring to a boil, and then remove from the heat. Pour the contents into a small sealable container and refrigerate it overnight.

3   When you're ready to use the pickled mustard seeds, scoop them from the brine, straining off any excess liquid.

Osso Buco with Lavender-Citrus Gremolata

SLOW COOKER SIZE: **6+ QUARTS**
SERVES **4**
PREP TIME: **20 MINUTES**
COOK TIME: **8 TO 12 HOURS**

This is a classic braise done right. Cross cuts of veal shank are slowly cooked to fall off the bone and balanced with the punch of gremolata. It is a quintessential Italian dish that succinctly shows why the simplicity of Italian food is so beautiful.

If osso buco were on OkCupid, its profile would read: "Fluent in Italian. Likes slow braising, a zesty finish, and a healthy side of polenta or grits."

4 cross-cut veal shanks (about 1 pound each, and 2 inches thick)

Kosher salt

¾ cup flour, preferably Wondra

1 tablespoon unsalted butter

3 tablespoons extra-virgin olive oil

1 large leek (white and light green parts), halved lengthwise, rinsed well, and cut into thin half-moons

1 large carrot, large-diced

2 celery stalks, large-diced

8 garlic cloves, smashed

1 cup dry white wine

1 tablespoon tomato paste

2 medium tomatoes, diced

4 bay leaves

2 sprigs fresh thyme

3 cups Beef Shin Stock (page 21) or Slow Cooker Chicken Broth (page 17)

½ cup Lavender-Citrus Gremolata (recipe follows)

1   Season the veal shanks all over with salt. Coat each shank with the flour on all sides, shaking off any excess. Place your largest skillet over medium heat and add the butter and olive oil. When the butter has melted, add the shanks to the pan. Brown on all sides for 10 minutes in total, until deep golden. Transfer the shanks to a slow cooker.

2   Add the leek, carrot, celery, and garlic to the skillet and sauté for 5 minutes, until the vegetables are beginning to soften. Then add the wine and deglaze the pan, scraping up the browned bits. Add the tomato paste, stir to dissolve it, then stir in the diced tomatoes. Season with salt to taste.

3   Pour the contents of the skillet into the slow cooker, add the bay leaves and thyme sprigs, then pour in the stock. Cover with the lid and cook on the low setting until tender, 8 to 12 hours, though they will probably be better at 12 hours than 8.

4   When the shanks are done, remove 2 cups of the cooking liquid. Strain the liquid into a small saucepan and place it over medium-high heat. When the liquid has reduced by half, remove from the heat, taste it, and add salt as needed.

5   Place each veal shank on a dinner plate and spoon some of the reduced sauce over it. Top with a hefty dollop of the Lavender-Citrus Gremolata, and serve.

LAVENDER-CITRUS GREMOLATA

MAKES ½ CUP

Grated zest of 1 medium orange

Grated zest of 2 medium lemons

1 garlic clove, finely minced

2 tablespoons finely chopped fresh flat-leaf parsley leaves

1 tablespoon minced fresh lavender leaves

2 tablespoons olive oil

Kosher salt

In a small bowl, stir together all the ingredients, seasoning the mixture with salt to taste. This can be made up to 2 days ahead and stored, covered, in the refrigerator.

Flank Steak with Guajillo Chiles & Cactus Salad

SLOW COOKER SIZE: **4+ QUARTS**
SERVES **4**
PREP TIME: **20 MINUTES**
COOK TIME: **2 HOURS**

Flank steak cooked this way—seared to give it that charred character and then slowly braised to absorb the beautiful cooking stock—is so good and simple. The finished dish is brightened even further with the cactus and the chiles. Make sure you slice the beef very thin, as that will ensure a tender bite.

1 flank steak (2 pounds), trimmed of fat and sinew

Kosher salt

2 teaspoons freshly ground black pepper

1 tablespoon extra-virgin olive oil

1 medium sweet onion, large-diced

2 garlic cloves, thinly sliced

6 dried guajillo chiles, soaked overnight, stemmed, seeded, and torn into large pieces

1 tablespoon cumin seeds, toasted and ground

1 quart Beef Shin Stock (page 21)

Cactus Salad (recipe follows)

1   Pat the steak dry and season it all over with salt and the black pepper. In a large skillet, heat the olive oil over medium heat. When the oil begins to shimmer, add the steak and sear it for 3 minutes on each side, until nicely browned. Remove the steak from the skillet and place it in a slow cooker. With the skillet still set over medium heat, add the onions and garlic and cook for 5 minutes, until softened. Remove the skillet from the heat, stir in the guajillos and cumin, and then scrape the contents into the slow cooker. Add the stock, cover with the lid, and cook on the low setting for 2 hours.

2   Transfer the steak to a cutting board and let it rest for a few minutes. Meanwhile, puree the braising mixture in the slow cooker with an immersion blender, or transfer it to a standing blender or a food processor and puree until smooth. Slice the steak thinly against the grain, and arrange the slices over the pureed sauce on individual plates. Sprinkle each slice with salt to taste. Garnish with the Cactus Salad.

CACTUS SALAD

You should be able to find cactus (called *nopales* or *nopalitos*) or prickly pear at a local Mexican *supermercado*. Find one and shop there often, or order the cactus online. Like okra, cactus has a pleasant gooeyness and a deep vegetal flavor.

SERVES 4 AS A SIDE

Kosher salt

½ pound nopales cactus or prickly pear

6 radishes, thinly sliced

4 tomatillos, small-diced

¼ cup coarsely chopped fresh cilantro, leaves and stems

2 tablespoons extra-virgin olive oil

¼ cup crumbled Cotija cheese

¼ cup freshly squeezed lime juice

1   Fill a large pot with water, bring it to a boil, and salt it. Fill a large bowl with ice and cold water and set it nearby.

2   With a knife, cut off any spines on the cactus and then cut it into thin, bite-size strips. Blanch the cactus in the boiling water for just a minute or two, until the cactus is bright green and slightly softened. Then immediately drain it and plunge it into the ice bath to stop the cooking. When the cactus has cooled, rinse off any excess goo under running water. Pat the cactus dry.

3   In a medium bowl, toss together the cactus, radishes, tomatillos, cilantro, olive oil, Cotija cheese, and lime juice. Refrigerate until ready to use. The salad will keep in the fridge, in a covered container, for a couple of days.

Classic Braised Short Ribs with Mashed Sweet Potatoes & Sweet Potato Greens

SLOW COOKER SIZE: **6+ QUARTS**

SERVES **6**

PREP TIME: **35 MINUTES**

COOK TIME: **12 TO 15 HOURS**

So good. So easy. Just make it happen. I like the "kosher cut" style of short rib, with the bones cut through, as opposed to the long cut of an "English cut."

6 pounds "kosher cut" bone-in short ribs, cut into 1-pound portions

Kosher salt

1 tablespoon freshly ground black pepper

2 tablespoons canola oil

1 large sweet onion, diced

4 garlic cloves, halved

10 dried juniper berries

4 sprigs fresh rosemary

½ cup port wine

Sweet Potato Greens with Lime and Ginger (recipe follows)

Mashed Sweet Potatoes (recipe follows)

1 Preheat a slow cooker on the low setting for at least 20 minutes.

2 Season the short ribs all over with salt and the pepper.

3 Heat the oil in a large heavy skillet over medium-high heat. When the oil is shimmering, sear the short ribs in it for 3 minutes on each meaty side, for a total of about 10 minutes, to get good color on them. Then transfer the short ribs to the slow cooker. Sear the beef in batches if necessary.

4 Add the onion, garlic, juniper berries, and rosemary sprigs to the skillet and cook for 3 minutes, until the onion is starting to soften. Add the port wine and remove the skillet from the heat. Stir gently, scraping up any browned bits, then pour the onion mixture into the slow cooker. Cover the cooker with the lid and cook on the low setting for 12 to 15 hours (don't stop cooking until that meat wants to fall off the bone).

5 Serve the short ribs on a platter with some of the braising liquid drizzled over them, and with Sweet Potato Greens and Mashed Sweet Potatoes on the side.

MASHED SWEET POTATOES

This classic sweet potato side is a quick and easy accompaniment to the rich short ribs. Make sure to buy real maple syrup to support your Vermont and Quebec farmers.

SERVES 6 AS A SIDE

4 large sweet potatoes

Kosher salt

¼ cup (½ stick) unsalted butter

¼ cup real maple syrup

Pinch of ground cayenne pepper

½ cup whole milk, warmed

Peel the sweet potatoes and cut them into 1-inch dice. Place the potatoes in a large pot, cover with cold water, and bring it to a boil. When the water is boiling, season it well with salt. Then reduce the heat and simmer for about 15 minutes, until the potatoes are tender. Drain the potatoes and return them to the pot. Mash with a masher or a ricer—a ricer will offer a much smoother consistency and the masher's results will be more rustic. Add the butter, maple syrup, cayenne, and milk. Whip well with a spoon and season with more salt to taste.

SWEET POTATO GREENS WITH LIME & GINGER

This recipe also works well with mustard greens—and really with any sturdy greens.

SERVES 6 AS A SIDE

1 tablespoon grapeseed oil

1 tablespoon minced fresh ginger

1 pound sweet potato greens

1 teaspoon unsalted butter

1 teaspoon freshly squeezed lime juice

½ teaspoon kosher salt

Place a large skillet over high heat and heat it for a couple of minutes. When the pan is hot, add the grapeseed oil; then add the ginger. Cook for 30 seconds, or until very aromatic, then add the greens. Cook, stirring, for 2 minutes or until softened. Add the butter and lime juice, stir well to combine, and season with the salt. Serve immediately.

PORCINE
DREAMS

IF HAM
COULD
FLY

There is so much good pork out there nowadays, and there is a massive difference between the flavor of pork raised and nurtured to be awesome and the flavor of commodity pork raised to be cheap. Be on the lookout for Duroc, Tamworth, Large Black, Red Wattle, Berkshire, and other heritage breeds from a good butcher or farmers' market. Visit with a farmer near you, chat a bit, and you'll see why what they do is so much better.

Milk-Braised Pork Shoulder with Fennel, Pecans & Figs

SLOW COOKER SIZE: **6+ QUARTS**
SERVES **6**
PREP TIME: **40 MINUTES**
COOK TIME: **8 TO 12 HOURS**

I love milk-braised pork. It is moist and succulent and really gives you a glimpse into the reality that Italians do not eat pasta at every meal and don't all have Ferraris. The diversity of the Italian food map is wonderful, and if you look at it you will see that braised dishes like this are a beautiful staple in the north. And they will often serve them up with some polenta.

Pork, milk, nuts, figs . . . this is such a deliciously savory poem.

3 pounds boneless pork shoulder

Kosher salt

2 teaspoons freshly ground black pepper

3 tablespoons olive oil

2 medium onions, diced

6 bay leaves

6 whole cloves

2 quarts whole milk

2 fennel bulbs

½ cup pecan halves, toasted and chopped

8 dried figs, thinly sliced

1 tablespoon freshly squeezed lemon juice

2 tablespoons chopped fresh flat-leaf parsley leaves

1   Preheat a slow cooker on the high setting for at least 15 minutes.

2   Pat the pork shoulder dry and season it well all over with salt and the pepper.

3   Heat 2 tablespoons of the olive oil in a large braising pot, such as a Dutch oven, over medium-high heat. When the oil is shimmering, add the pork and sear it for about 3 minutes on each side until golden, for a total of about 12 minutes.

4   Remove the pork from the pot and set it aside. Add the onions, bay leaves, cloves, and milk to the pot and cook, scraping up any browned bits, for 3 minutes.

(recipe continues)

5   Add the milk mixture to the slow cooker,
    then add the pork. Cover with the lid,
    reduce the setting to low, and cook for 8 to
    12 hours, until the pork is very tender.

6   Before serving the pork, prepare the fennel
    by removing the bottom ½ inch of the root
    ends and cutting away the branches about
    1 inch above the bulbs. Cut the bulbs in half
    lengthwise and then into thirds.

7   Heat the remaining tablespoon of olive oil
    in a large skillet over medium heat. Add the
    fennel pieces, season them well with salt,
    and cook for 5 minutes, until caramelized.
    Then flip the pieces over and cook until
    done, about 5 minutes more. Remove the
    fennel from the skillet and set it aside. Add
    the pecans and figs to the skillet and cook
    for 3 minutes. Stir in the lemon juice and
    chopped parsley, and immediately transfer
    the mixture to a small bowl.

8   Remove the pork shoulder from the slow
    cooker and place it on a platter. Arrange
    the fennel around the pork, and garnish the
    dish with the pecan and fig crumble. The
    pork will be so tender that you don't really
    have to carve it—you can just pull it apart
    and serve it.

Slow Cooker Bo Ssam

SLOW COOKER SIZE: **6+ QUARTS**
SERVES **10 TO 12** (GREAT FOR A DINNER PARTY!)
PREP TIME: **15 MINUTES**
COOK TIME: **10 TO 15 HOURS**

Here's some good old-fashioned cultural appropriation for you: I have never been to Korea. I have driven a rental Hyundai, though, and eaten a fair bit of Korean food. This is my take on *bo ssam*, slow cooker style. *Bo ssam* is the epitome of family-style eating. The succulent pork is torn and placed in a lettuce leaf and garnished to your liking with spicy, funky sauces and crisp pickles, and everyone (of age) imbibes a cold lager. The world knows what we are talking about when we talk *bo ssam* because of the wunderkind that is the NYC-based chef David Chang. Respect.

1 bone-in pork shoulder (5 to 7 pounds)

Kosher salt

2 tablespoons vegetable oil

1 tablespoon light brown sugar

1 teaspoon crushed red pepper flakes

"Chang-ian" Sauces (recipes follow)

Freshly shucked oysters, as many as you can afford

2 cups cabbage kimchi, coarsely chopped

2 heads tender lettuce, such as Bibb or butter lettuce, separated into whole leaves

Seasonal pickles, such as pickled turnips, cucumbers, radishes, or carrots (or whatever you have on hand), for serving

1   Pat the pork shoulder dry and season it well all over with salt.

2   Place a large skillet or Dutch oven over medium-high heat and add the oil. When the oil begins to shimmer, add the pork shoulder and sear it on all sides, starting with the fatty side, for about 5 minutes per side, until nicely browned. Transfer the pork to a slow cooker with the fat cap facing up. Sprinkle the brown sugar and red pepper flakes over the pork, cover the cooker with the lid, and cook on the low setting for 10 hours, until very tender; it can cook for up to 15 hours if you'd like.

3   To serve, remove the pork from the cooker and set it aside to cool slightly. Place the two sauces, oysters, kimchi, lettuce leaves, and pickles in separate serving vessels. Pull or slice the pork (it will let you know which it prefers) and arrange it on a platter. Instruct your guests to use a lettuce leaf like a taco shell and fill it with some pork, kimchi, sauces, some pickles, and an oyster. And provide plenty of napkins. It's a tasty mess.

"CHANG-IAN" SAUCE A (SSAM SAUCE)

Gochujang and doenjang can be purchased from any Korean grocery store and most Asian markets.

MAKES 1¼ CUPS

¼ cup gochujang (Korean chile paste)

½ cup doenjang (Korean soybean paste)

¼ cup cider vinegar

In a small bowl, whisk together all the ingredients, thinning the mixture with ¼ cup water. The sauce will keep, refrigerated, for many moons.

"CHANG-IAN" SAUCE B (SCALLION SAUCE)

MAKES ABOUT 1½ CUPS

2 bunches scallions (white and light green parts only), thinly sliced

2 tablespoons minced fresh ginger

3 tablespoons soy sauce

¼ cup grapeseed or other neutral oil

3 tablespoons rice vinegar

1 tablespoon sesame seeds

1 teaspoon sesame oil

In a small bowl, stir all the ingredients together. The sauce will keep, refrigerated, for about 1 week.

Beer-Braised Pork Tacos

This is one of those dishes that will feed a lot of drunk (or sober) people really well. It is easy and redeeming. Feel free to garnish the tacos further as you wish, maybe with avocado, lime, some Cotija cheese, and charred scallions.

8 pounds bone-in pork shoulder

Kosher salt

1 tablespoon freshly ground black pepper

2 tablespoons olive oil

1 cup lard

3 small onions: 1 large-diced, 2 minced

2 garlic cloves, thinly sliced

2 teaspoons coriander seeds, toasted and ground

½ teaspoon ground cinnamon

3 tablespoons freshly squeezed lime juice

1 (6.5-ounce) can chipotle peppers in adobo sauce

1 (12-ounce) can of simple beer

Canola oil

24 white corn tortillas

2 cups crumbled Cotija cheese

4 limes, cut into wedges

Tomatillo Salsa Verde (recipe follows)

1   Preheat a large slow cooker on the low setting for at least 20 minutes.

2   Pat the pork shoulder dry with paper towels and season it very well all over with salt and the pepper. Place a large skillet over medium-high heat, add the olive oil, and when the oil is shimmering, add the pork shoulder and sear it for 5 minutes per side, until golden. Transfer the pork to the slow cooker.

3   Reduce the heat to medium and add the lard to the skillet. Once it has melted, add the large-diced onion and the garlic; cook for 5 minutes, until softening. Add this to the slow cooker, along with the coriander, cinnamon, lime juice, chipotle in adobo, and the beer. Cover with the lid and cook on the low setting for 12 hours while you drink the remaining cans of beer that came in your six-pack.

4   Place a large skillet over medium heat and add a touch of canola oil. Griddle the tortillas, one or two at a time, for a few seconds per side until warmed through and toasty. As you process through the tortillas, stack and place them in a resealable plastic bag to stay warm.

5   Put the braised pork in a serving vessel and serve with the warm tortillas, minced onion, Cotija, lime wedges, and Tomatillo Salsa Verde, plus any other toppings you love on a taco.

TOMATILLO SALSA VERDE

MAKES 2 CUPS

6 to 8 tomatillos, coarsely chopped (2 cups)

1 small sweet onion, large-diced

1 packed cup fresh cilantro stems and leaves

2 tablespoons freshly squeezed lime juice

1 teaspoon ground cumin

1½ tablespoons thinly sliced seeded serrano chiles

1 tablespoon extra-virgin olive oil

Kosher salt

Combine the tomatillos, onion, cilantro, lime juice, cumin, chiles, and olive oil in a blender and puree until smooth. Season with salt to taste. This can be prepared ahead of time, and will keep refrigerated for up to 1 week.

Tripe & Bacon Stew with Borlotti Beans & Tomatillo Salsa Verde

SLOW COOKER SIZE: 4+ QUARTS
SERVES 6
PREP TIME: 40 MINUTES
COOK TIME: 2 HOURS, BUT IT CAN GO LONGER IF NEEDED

Tripe is one of those things that are repulsive to many people, but when it's done right, it just is so darned good. The key is finding good tripe and cooking it well. First, locate a place that sells a lot of it. For me, that is the Mexican grocery store off of Chase Street in my hometown of Athens, Georgia. The Mexican culinary culture has a love for tripe, so this grocery moves a lot of it. You might also find it in an Asian market or at a good butcher shop. Make sure it is washed well and is very fresh. I get the best results with honeycomb tripe, but any tripe will do if it is very clean. Tripe tenderizes beautifully through a long cook in your slow cooker.

¾ pound honeycomb tripe

¾ pound dried borlotti beans

¾ pound slab bacon, large-diced

1 large sweet onion, large-diced

3 garlic cloves, thinly sliced

½ pound plum tomatoes, small-diced

1½ quarts Slow Cooker Chicken Broth (page 17)

1 large celery stalk, small-diced

2 teaspoons salt

2 teaspoons ground white pepper

½ teaspoon ground cayenne pepper, or to taste

1½ tablespoons finely chopped fresh thyme leaves

1 cup Tomatillo Salsa Verde (page 207)

1   Place the tripe in a large pot, cover with cold water, and bring the water to a boil. Reduce the heat to a simmer and cook for 30 minutes, or until the tripe is easily pierced with a knife. Drain the tripe and chop it into bite-size pieces. Soak the tripe pieces in a bowl of cold water until ready to use.

2   Pour the beans into the same pot and add water to cover by 3 inches. Bring the water to a boil, boil for 5 minutes, and then pour the beans and 4 cups of the cooking water into a slow cooker.

3   In a large skillet set over medium heat, cook the bacon for 5 minutes, until rendered. Add the onion, garlic, and tripe (drained and soaking water discarded) and cook for 5 minutes more, to coat well. Transfer the bacon mixture to the slow cooker. Add the tomatoes, broth, celery, salt, white pepper, cayenne, and thyme, and cook on the low setting for 2 hours.

4   Scoop the stew into individual bowls and garnish each one with a big ol' dollop of Tomatillo Salsa Verde.

Pseudo BBQ Pork Ribs

These are the kind of ribs you find at the grocery store. They are not precious, because this is not precious food, but they are tasty. Less sweet and ketchup-laden than most ribs in this style, the pork ends up just falling off the bone, and the gochujang, a Korean chile paste available at Asian markets, brings a lot of umami to the plate.

Why do I call them "pseudo"? 'Cause real barbecue has smoke and fire. This doesn't. This is easy. Get them going and walk away.

Serve whatever makes you feel good with these ribs: some red beans and rice, tangy cole slaw, a big tomato salad (see page 180), and some ice-cold beer . . . oh, and cornbread.

6 pounds pork spareribs

Blender BBQ Sauce (recipe follows)

4 sprigs fresh thyme

1   The 6 pounds of ribs will probably be pre-portioned into 2 slabs. Cut each one in half, running a knife parallel to the bones in the middle, creating 4 half-slabs. Pat the ribs dry with paper towels and place them in a large mixing bowl. Pour the barbecue sauce over the ribs and mix them up a bit to coat.

2   In a large slow cooker, line up the rib half-slabs vertically as if they were file folders and the slow cooker a file cabinet drawer, adding the thyme sprigs between the layers. Scrape any sauce remaining in the bowl over the ribs. Set the cooker on the low setting, cover with the lid, and cook for 8 hours.

3   Preheat the oven to 400°F.

4   Carefully remove the ribs from the cooker and place them in a single layer on a baking sheet. Brush any barbecue sauce left in the cooker over the cooked ribs, and then roast them in the oven for 10 minutes to brown. Then they're ready to eat!

BLENDER BBQ SAUCE

MAKES 2 CUPS

2 tablespoons unsalted butter

1 medium sweet onion, diced

3 garlic cloves, halved

1 (14-ounce) can plum tomatoes, drained

¼ cup packed light brown sugar

2 tablespoons Worcestershire sauce

1 cup cider vinegar

2 tablespoons gochujang (Korean chile paste)

1 tablespoon yellow mustard

1 teaspoon kosher salt

½ teaspoon freshly
ground black pepper

1   Place a medium skillet over medium heat. Add the butter, and when it bubbles and froths, add the onion and garlic. Cook for 15 minutes, stirring often, until very soft and caramelized.

2   Place the cooked onion and the tomatoes, sugar, Worcestershire, vinegar, gochujang, mustard, salt, and pepper in a blender. Blend until smooth. This will keep, refrigerated, for up to 1 week.

Pork Belly Choucroute Garnie

SLOW COOKER SIZE: **4+ QUARTS**
SERVES **6 TO 8**
PREP TIME: **20 MINUTES**
COOK TIME: **10 TO 15 HOURS**

Choucroute garnie literally translates to "garnished sauerkraut," but it's much more impressive than the name suggests. It's a debaucherous Alsatian feast of fermented cabbage loaded with sausages, roast pork, braised pork, smoked pork, pig in all its forms. In this preparation, we've simplified it to "just" a tender, rich braised pork belly, but you could add some nice pork sausages and some grilled chops if you want to get really serious.

¼ cup cider vinegar

Kosher salt

2 pounds pork belly, skin removed

4 bay leaves

4 sprigs fresh thyme

1 tablespoon allspice berries

1 tablespoon black peppercorns

Sauerkraut and Apples (recipe follows)

Apple slices, for garnish

1   Preheat a slow cooker on the low setting for at least 20 minutes.

2   In a medium pot, combine 2 quarts water with the cider vinegar and 2 tablespoons salt (or to taste), and bring to a boil over high heat. Then pour the liquid into the slow cooker. Add the pork belly, bay leaves, thyme sprigs, allspice berries, and peppercorns. Cover with the lid and cook on the low setting for 10 hours, until the belly is very tender. You can cook it up to 15 hours if you'd like.

3   Spoon the Sauerkraut and Apples onto a platter, arrange the pork belly over the top, and garnish with nice apple slices. The pork will be fairly tender to slice into individual portions.

SAUERKRAUT AND APPLES

SERVES 8

½ cup small-diced slab bacon

2 small sweet onions, large-diced

2 cups dry white wine

4 pounds prepared sauerkraut

2 large apples, cored and small-diced

½ cup fresh flat-leaf parsley leaves

Kosher salt and freshly ground black pepper

Place a large skillet over medium-high heat, add the bacon, and cook for 4 minutes, until rendered and starting to crisp. Add the onions and cook for 3 minutes, until translucent. Then add the white wine and cook, scraping up the browned bits with a spoon, for 3 minutes or until most of the liquid has reduced. Add the sauerkraut and apples, and cook for another 3 minutes. Then remove the pan from the heat and stir in the parsley. Season to taste with salt and pepper.

LAMB & GOAT

Goat farming has come a long way. Goat is now a treat, thanks to better animal husbandry. It has lost that gamey tang and now has a closer kinship to lamb than the goat of yore. You can find it more readily these days, so try it out—you won't be disappointed. As for lamb, I think true North American lamb is the best lamb in the world—especially when raised by farmers like the folks at Jamison Farm in Pennsylvania and Border Springs Farm in Virginia. Goat and lamb are great meats to expand the parameters of your slow cooker thinking. They love low and slow.

Lamb Pozole

Pozole is a soup or a stew—define it as you'd like. More than that, it is a beautiful dish, warming souls with brightness and richness, spicy but soothing. This recipe is the perfect one-pot meal, full of flavors—chiles, cumin, cinnamon, beans, and corn—that harmonize to make a really beautiful dinner. It is an effort worth making. Serve the pozole with some crisp tortillas (see page 68) on the side. And a beer. With a lime in it.

8 dried guajillo chiles

4 lamb hind shanks (about 1 pound each)

Kosher salt

1 teaspoon freshly ground black pepper

¼ cup vegetable oil

1 large red onion: half large-diced, half minced

1 head unpeeled garlic, halved horizontally

6 carrots: 2 large-diced, 4 minced

8 celery stalks: 2 large-diced, 6 minced

2 teaspoons cumin seeds, toasted and ground

1 (2-inch) piece of cinnamon stick

2 tablespoons fresh oregano leaves, chopped

3 quarts Slow Cooker Chicken Broth (page 17)

¼ cup olive oil

3 cups canned hominy, drained and rinsed

2 cups canned pinto beans, drained and rinsed

1 teaspoon coriander seeds, toasted and ground

½ cup chopped fresh cilantro leaves and stems

1 lime, quartered

1 avocado, pitted, peeled, and sliced

1   Preheat a slow cooker on the low setting for at least 20 minutes.

2   Coarsely chop 4 of the guajillo chiles into 1-inch-long pieces, discarding the stems; set aside.

3   Pat the lamb shanks dry with paper towels and season them all over with salt and the black pepper. In a large braising pan, heat the oil over medium-high heat. Add the shanks and sear them for 5 minutes per side, until nicely browned. Remove the shanks from the pan and set them aside.

4   Add the large-diced onion, the halved head of garlic, and the large-diced carrots and celery to the pan and reduce the heat to medium. Cook for 5 minutes, until the vegetables are starting to soften. Then add half of the cumin, the cinnamon stick, the oregano, and the coarsely chopped guajillo chiles. Add the broth and bring to a boil.

(recipe continues)

5 Place the seared shanks in the slow cooker, then carefully add the boiling broth and aromatics. Cover the cooker with the lid and cook on the low setting for 8 hours, until very tender. (You can cook it for up to 12 hours if you'd like.) Skim off any fat that rises to the surface.

6 About 1½ hours before you want to serve the lamb, place the remaining 4 guajillo chiles in a bowl of warm water to cover and let them soak for 30 minutes. Then drain the chiles, reserving 1 cup of the soaking liquid. Place the chiles and the reserved soaking liquid in a blender or food processor, and puree. Set the puree aside.

7 When the lamb shanks are cooked, warm the olive oil in a large skillet over medium-high heat. Add the minced onion, minced carrots, minced celery, a pinch of salt, and the hominy and pinto beans. Cook for 5 minutes, until hot. Then add the remaining cumin and the coriander. Add the guajillo puree to the vegetables and beans, and then transfer everything to the slow cooker. Cook for 30 minutes to 1 hour on the low setting to integrate the flavors. Turn off the heat, stir in the chopped cilantro, and season to taste with additional salt.

8 Ladle the pozole into bowls, garnishing each serving with a lime wedge and some slices of avocado.

Lamb Shanks with Medjool Dates, Orange & Za'atar

SLOW COOKER SIZE: **6+ QUARTS**
SERVES **4**
PREP TIME: **40 MINUTES**
COOK TIME: **12 TO 15 HOURS**

For this dish, you are looking at one lamb shank per person. Then I need you to watch *Casablanca*, read *The Sheltering Sky*, and brush up on your Middle Eastern political history, as this recipe honors that semicircle fronting the Mediterranean Sea from Morocco to Beirut. This takes a day to make, but it is a day of filling your house with the smells of slow-cooking lamb, pungent citrus, za'atar, and plump dates. In my mind, that is a good day.

A note on za'atar: It is a tart, aromatic, savory Middle Eastern spice blend. It is wonderful. And it is easy to make if you can't find it: Combine 2 tablespoons chopped fresh thyme leaves with ¼ cup toasted sesame seeds, 1 teaspoon sea salt, and 2 tablespoons ground sumac. Mix it up. It will stay fresh for a couple of days in the fridge but is best when used as soon as possible.

4 lamb hind shanks (about 1 pound each)

Kosher salt

Freshly ground black pepper

2 tablespoons vegetable oil

2 medium yellow onions, quartered

4 garlic cloves, halved

1 medium orange, scrubbed

1 (2-inch) piece of cinnamon stick

2 star anise pods

1 teaspoon coriander seeds

¼ teaspoon crushed red pepper flakes

½ cup red wine vinegar

1 quart Slow Cooker Chicken Broth (page 17)

12 Medjool dates, pitted

¼ cup za'atar

Fresh mint leaves (optional)

(recipe continues)

1   Pat the lamb shanks dry with paper towels and season them well all over with salt and 1 tablespoon pepper. Place a large skillet over medium heat and warm the vegetable oil in it until it begins to shimmer. Then add the lamb shanks, in batches if necessary, and sauté them for 5 minutes per side, until nicely browned. Transfer the shanks to a slow cooker and turn the cooker to the low setting.

2   Add the onions and garlic to the same skillet, still over medium heat, and cook for 5 minutes, until slightly softened. Add them to the slow cooker.

3   Remove the orange zest with a grater (such as a Microplane) and add 2 teaspoons of the grated zest to the cooker. (Set the remaining orange aside for later.) Add the cinnamon stick, star anise pods, coriander seeds, red pepper flakes, vinegar, and broth to the slow cooker, cover with the lid, and cook for 12 hours on the low setting, until very tender. (You can cook it for up to 15 hours if you'd like.)

4   Remove 2 cups of the liquid from the slow cooker and pour it into a small pot. Place the pot over medium-high heat and cook until the liquid has reduced by half, about 10 minutes. Reduce the heat to medium-low, add the dates to the reduction, and cook them for 3 minutes.

5   With a sharp paring knife, remove the remaining pith from the orange and segment the orange into supremes by running the knife carefully between each segment and its membrane to release the fruit. (Do this to 100 oranges in an hour and I will employ you happily.)

6   Carefully place the lamb shanks on a platter, trying to keep them intact, and get those onion pieces nestling up with the shanks. Pour the dates and the date reduction over the top. Garnish with the orange supremes, the za'atar, and a few mint leaves, if you like, and serve.

Leg of Lamb with Classic Salsa Verde

SLOW COOKER SIZE: **6+ QUARTS**
SERVES **4 TO 6**
PREP TIME: **35 MINUTES**
COOK TIME: **2¼ HOURS**

So simple but so succulent, this leg of lamb is cooked until medium or medium-rare in the slow cooker and is perfect for a Saturday: the results will give you lamb for dinner, and for sandwiches the next day. If you don't have a spring lamb weekend in May, then you are just missing out on one of the glories of cooking.

1 bone-in leg of lamb (about 4 pounds)

Kosher salt

1 teaspoon freshly ground black pepper

2 tablespoons olive oil

1 large onion, sliced into 1-inch-thick rounds

2 sprigs fresh rosemary

4 bay leaves

8 garlic cloves, smashed

1 cup dry white wine

1 quart Slow Cooker Chicken Broth (page 17)

Classic Salsa Verde (recipe follows)

1 Preheat a large slow cooker on the high setting for at least 15 minutes.

2 Pat the lamb dry with paper towels and season it all over with salt and the pepper.

3 Place a large skillet over medium-high heat. Add the olive oil and when it is shimmering, add the lamb and carefully sear it for 5 minutes, until golden brown. Turn the lamb over and sear the other side for 5 minutes. Remove the lamb from the pan and place it in the slow cooker.

4 Add the onion, rosemary, bay leaves, garlic, white wine, and broth to the slow cooker. Cover the cooker with the lid and cook on the high setting for 2¼ hours, until the meat is a nice pink—medium or medium-rare. Remove the lamb and let it rest for 20 minutes prior to slicing.

5 Slice the lamb very thin and serve it warm, room temperature, or cold (you pick!), with the salsa verde alongside.

CLASSIC SALSA VERDE

MAKES 2 CUPS

½ cup packed fresh flat-leaf parsley leaves, finely chopped

1 tablespoon finely chopped fresh basil leaves

1 tablespoon finely chopped fresh mint leaves

1 tablespoon finely chopped fresh marjoram leaves

¾ cup olive oil, plus more to taste

2 garlic cloves, minced

Pinch of crushed red pepper flakes

1 tablespoon salt-packed capers, rinsed well and chopped

1 tablespoon salt-packed anchovy fillets, rinsed and minced

1 teaspoon Dijon mustard

1 tablespoon cider vinegar or white wine vinegar

Kosher salt and freshly ground black pepper

Place the parsley, basil, mint, and marjoram in a medium bowl and pour in the ¾ cup olive oil. Add the garlic, red pepper flakes, capers, and anchovies. Stir well. Then add the mustard and the vinegar. Season with salt and pepper to taste, and thin with more olive oil if necessary. The salsa will keep in the refrigerator for up to 5 days.

Goat & Garlic
with Jeweled Couscous

SLOW COOKER SIZE: **6+ QUARTS**

SERVES **8**

PREP TIME: **30 MINUTES**

COOK TIME: **12 TO 15 HOURS**

Goat is a special thing, and it is a food that we should be eating more of. It has a reputation for being gamey and strong, but I have found that the way it is being raised today, and the breeds that good goat farmers are using, has really made that a bygone trait. This dish reminds me of North Africa, with lots of garlic, coriander, and oregano. I serve it with couscous because I love couscous jeweled with nuts, apricots, and parsley. If you can't get a beautiful goat shoulder, lamb would also be delicious here.

1 bone-in goat shoulder (about 5 pounds)

Kosher salt

1 tablespoon freshly ground black pepper

3 tablespoons olive oil

12 garlic cloves, thinly sliced

2 sweet onions, quartered

2 quarts Beef Shin Stock (page 21)

2 medium carrots, large-diced

½ pound tomato, large-diced

2 teaspoons coriander seeds, toasted and ground

1 lemon, halved

4 bay leaves

2 tablespoons honey

2 tablespoons coarsely chopped fresh oregano leaves

Jeweled Couscous (recipe follows)

1   Pat the goat shoulder dry with paper towels and season it well all over with salt and the pepper.

2   Heat the olive oil in a large skillet over medium heat. When the oil begins to shimmer, add the goat and sear it for 5 minutes on each side to get good color. Transfer it to a slow cooker.

3   Add the garlic to the skillet and cook for 3 minutes, until very aromatic and golden brown; transfer it to the slow cooker. Add the onions, stock, carrots, tomato, coriander, lemon, and bay leaves to the cooker. Season with salt to taste, cover the cooker with the lid, and cook on the low setting for 12 to 15 hours, until the meat is very tender.

4   Stir the honey into the meat mixture, top with oregano, and serve it with a side of couscous.

JEWELED COUSCOUS

This is just one way to dress up your couscous. You could also add any nuts, herbs, dried fruits, pickles, crumbled cheeses (such as feta), yogurt, and so on that you'd like.

SERVES 8 AS A SIDE

2 tablespoons unsalted butter

2 cups Vegetable Stock (page 27; water or other stocks will work too)

2 cups fine, Moroccan-style couscous

2 tablespoons olive oil

1⅓ cups pecan halves, toasted

2 cups small-diced dried apricots

2 teaspoons grated lemon zest

¼ cup coarsely chopped fresh flat-leaf parsley leaves

Kosher salt

Place the butter and the stock in a medium pot, bring to a boil, then remove the pot from the heat and whisk in the couscous. Cover the pot with a lid and set it aside for 20 minutes, until the couscous has absorbed all of the stock. Then add the olive oil and fluff the grains with a fork. Add the pecans, apricots, lemon zest, and parsley, gently stirring them into the couscous, and season with salt to taste. Serve.

Birria: Mexican Goat Stew

SLOW COOKER SIZE: **6+ QUARTS**
SERVES **8 TO 10**
PREP TIME: **15 MINUTES**
COOK TIME: **10 TO 15 HOURS**

Birria is a traditional Mexican stew made for a celebration. It should be served with tortillas, onions, cilantro, a salsa or two, and some freshly cut limes. You could make it with lamb if you want, but sometimes tracking down a goat is a fun project all by itself. Go find your goat.

5 pounds boneless goat, cut into large stewing pieces, about 1-inch cubes

Kosher salt

1 tablespoon freshly ground black pepper

2 tablespoons canola oil

2½ medium onions: 2 small-diced, 1 minced

6 garlic cloves, thinly sliced

2 dried guajillo chiles

2 red bell peppers, seeded and quartered

1 (6.5-ounce) can chipotle peppers in adobo sauce

½ pound tomatoes, small-diced

4 bay leaves

4 sprigs fresh oregano, plus 3 tablespoons coarsely chopped leaves

1 tablespoon cumin seeds, toasted and ground

¼ cup red wine vinegar

1 cup Slow Cooker Chicken Broth (page 17)

2 limes, quartered

Warmed tortillas, for serving

1   Pat the goat pieces dry with paper towels and season them all over with salt and the pepper.

2   Heat the canola oil in a large skillet over medium-high heat. When the oil is shimmering, add the goat meat and sear it for 3 minutes on each side, until golden brown, about 10 minutes total. Transfer the meat to a paper towel–lined plate. Add the diced onion and the garlic to the skillet and cook for 3 minutes, until translucent.

3   Place the goat meat in a slow cooker and add the cooked onion and garlic, as well as the guajillos, red bell peppers, chipotle in adobo, tomato, bay leaves, oregano sprigs, cumin, red wine vinegar, and broth. Cover with the lid and cook on the low setting for 10 hours, until very tender. (It may cook for up to 15 hours.)

4   Remove the cooked goat meat and the bay leaves and oregano sprigs from the slow cooker. Using an immersion blender, blend the remaining contents in the slow cooker (you can also transfer the contents to a blender or food processor to puree them). Return the cooked goat meat to the pureed sauce in the slow cooker.

5   Serve the stew in bowls, topped with the minced onion and the chopped oregano leaves, and garnished with lime wedges. Pass the tortillas.

Jams, fruit butters, preserves, and chutneys were built for slow cooking. They like long cook times with as little chance of burning in the pot as possible, and that's exactly what the slow cooker does best. If you want to can these, you will have to transfer the finished product to sterilized jars and process them in a hot water bath or a pressure canner, but that is up to you. All of them will stay fresh in the fridge for several weeks if you don't take that step.

These are all versatile recipes to add to your larder. Use them in different ways: fig jam and goat cheese make a beautiful sandwich; plum chutney is a stunner on a pork chop with sautéed spinach alongside. Or just on toast. I love toast.

TOAST IS READY.

HOW TO USE JAM

TOAST

Plum Chutney

SLOW COOKER SIZE: **4 QUARTS**
MAKES **1½ QUARTS**
PREP TIME: **20 MINUTES**
COOK TIME: **6 TO 8 HOURS**

This makes a great pair for cheese of all types. Or spread it on a turkey sandwich. Or on a biscuit with ham. Or spoon it over ice cream.

2 tablespoons extra-virgin olive oil

1 red onion, small-diced

1 cup sugar

1 teaspoon mustard seeds

½ teaspoon ground cloves

½ teaspoon ground cinnamon

3 pounds red plums, skin left on, small-diced

¼ cup red wine vinegar

2 teaspoons Dijon mustard

2 teaspoons Pickled Mustard Seeds (page 183)

1 Turn a slow cooker to the low setting.

2 Warm a small skillet over medium heat, and add the olive oil and diced red onion. Sweat the onion for 5 minutes, until softened. Remove from the heat and set aside.

3 In a large mixing bowl, combine the sugar, mustard seeds, cloves, cinnamon, and diced plums. Toss well, then transfer the mixture to the slow cooker. Add the onion and the red wine vinegar.

4 Cover with the lid and cook on the low setting for 6 to 8 hours, until the plums have melted.

5 Fold the Dijon mustard and pickled mustard seeds into the cooked plums. Let the chutney cool, and then store it in clean jars in the refrigerator.

6 The chutney will keep in the fridge for a couple of weeks, or you could fully process it in sterilized jars according to the jar manufacturer's instructions and have it be shelf-stable for up to a year.

Peach Butter

I live in the Peach State, so here is a peach butter recipe. It's a long cook, but it's worth it. Spread it on toast, or serve it with all things pork, like a modern version of applesauce.

1 cup dry vermouth

5 pounds peaches

1 cup sugar

1 teaspoon salt

1 (2-inch) piece of cinnamon stick

2 tablespoons unsalted butter

1 Preheat a slow cooker on the low setting for at least 20 minutes.

2 Add the vermouth to the preheated cooker.

3 Dice the peaches, keeping the skins on but discarding the pits. In a large bowl, toss the peaches with the sugar and salt; then transfer the peaches to the slow cooker. Add the cinnamon stick, cover with the lid, and cook on the low setting for 18 hours, until the peaches are a brown, goopy goodness.

4 Remove the cinnamon stick and then, using a slotted spoon to drain them of any liquid, transfer the peaches to a blender or food processor. Add the butter and puree until smooth. Let the puree cool, and then store it in clean jars in the refrigerator.

5 The peach butter will keep in the fridge for a couple of weeks, or you could fully process it in sterilized jars according to the jar manufacturer's instructions and have it be shelf-stable for up to a year.

Apple Cardamom Butter

I love apple butter. It is a breakfast staple in my house. The cardamom in this one adds a beautiful complexity and nuance that brings it to a new level. If you want to double the recipe and then jar it up for gifts, go right ahead . . . no one ever turns down the gift of apple butter.

5 pounds crisp red apples, such as Fuji or Gala

3 cups packed light brown sugar

¼ cup (½ stick) unsalted butter

1 teaspoon ground black cardamom

2 tablespoons American whiskey, such as Jack Daniel's

1 Preheat a slow cooker on the low setting for at least 20 minutes.

2 Meanwhile, peel and core the apples, then slice them thinly. In a large bowl, toss the apple slices with the brown sugar; set aside.

3 Add the butter to the preheated slow cooker. Once it has melted, stir in the cardamom and whiskey.

4 Add the apples to the slow cooker, stirring to combine everything. Cover with the lid and cook on the low setting for 18 to 24 hours, until a thick spread forms.

5 Transfer the apples to a blender or food processor, using a slotted spoon to drain them of any liquid, and puree until smooth. Let the puree cool, and then store it in clean jars in the refrigerator.

6 The apple butter will keep in the fridge for a couple of weeks, or you could fully process it in sterilized jars according to the jar manufacturer's instructions and have it be shelf-stable for up to a year.

Fig Jam

I have a small fig tree in my yard (our climate is pretty awesome for figs). That little tree is a bountiful fruiter and yields about eight gallons of super-sweet tiny little figs, which means we have to find ways to use them up. Fig jam is a great and tasty way to do just that.

4 quarts fresh figs, stemmed and quartered

2 cups honey

¼ cup freshly squeezed lemon juice

2 teaspoons freshly grated nutmeg

1   Preheat a slow cooker on the high setting for at least 15 minutes.

2   Add all the ingredients to the slow cooker. Cover with the lid and cook on the high setting for 3 hours.

3   Strain the fig mixture into a bowl. Reserve the juices that you strained off and put the solids into a blender. Puree the solids to the desired consistency, thinning with the juices as necessary. I like looser jams than most out there—they taste fresher to me. Let the jam cool, and then store it in clean jars in the refrigerator.

4   The fig jam will keep in the fridge for a couple of weeks, or you could fully process it in sterilized jars according to the jar manufacturer's instructions and have it be shelf-stable for up to a year.

Strawberry Rhubarb Jam

SLOW COOKER SIZE: **4+ QUARTS**

MAKES **2 QUARTS**

PREP TIME: **15 MINUTES PLUS 2 HOURS MACERATING**

COOK TIME: **3 HOURS**

This is the classic pairing of strawberries and rhubarb. Serve it on toast with some fresh cheese and black pepper ground over. Yum.

2 pounds strawberries, stemmed and hulled

2 pounds rhubarb stalks

2 cups sugar

2 tablespoons freshly squeezed lemon juice

1 vanilla bean, halved, seeds scraped out, pod and seeds reserved

1　Cut the strawberries into small dice. Cut the rhubarb stalks crosswise into thin slices. Place the strawberries and rhubarb in a slow cooker and toss with the sugar. Cover and let sit for 2 hours to macerate without turning on the cooker.

2　Turn the cooker to the high setting, and add the lemon juice and the vanilla bean (pod and seeds) to the fruit. Cover the cooker and cook for 3 hours, stirring often, until jammy and delicious. Let the jam cool, remove the vanilla bean pods, then store the jam in clean jars in the refrigerator.

3　The jam will keep in the fridge for a couple of weeks, or you could fully process it in sterilized jars according to the jar manufacturer's instructions and have it be shelf-stable for up to a year.

Muscadine Jelly

SLOW COOKER SIZE: **4+ QUARTS**
MAKES **1 QUART**
PREP TIME: **15 MINUTES**
COOK TIME: **3 HOURS**

I have a scuppernong (bronze/green) vine and a muscadine (black/purple) vine in my backyard. In late August or early September, they give off a bevy of grapes. This is the staple we proudly make from our bounty. You could make the same thing with Concord grapes, or other local grapes of your choice.

1 pound muscadine grapes

2 cups sugar

2 teaspoons citric acid

2 tablespoons powdered pectin

1 Preheat a slow cooker on the high setting for at least 15 minutes.

2 In a large bowl, toss together the grapes, sugar, and citric acid. Transfer the mixture to the slow cooker, cover with the lid, and cook on the high setting for 2 hours.

3 Pour the contents of the cooker through a fine-mesh strainer set over a large bowl. Using a spoon, smoosh the grapes through the strainer until only the seeds and skins are left. Discard the seeds and skins and return the strained liquid to the slow cooker. Whisk in the pectin, cover, and cook on the high setting for 1 hour.

4 Remove the mixture from the slow cooker and let it cool to room temperature. Then pack it in jars and chill them in the refrigerator to allow the jelly to set up, at least 1 hour. We are looking for it to be easily spoonable but to hold on for dear life to that spoon. When it's ready, make a PB&J.

5 The grape jelly will keep in the fridge for a few weeks.

Mexican-Style Sipping Chocolate

SLOW COOKER SIZE: **4 QUARTS**
MAKES **2 QUARTS**
PREP TIME: **2 MINUTES**
COOK TIME: **3 HOURS**

This beverage, great to make and hold in the slow cooker for a cold day or for a party, strikes a balance between sweet and spicy, a relationship that I love. It is a precarious balance, though, and may be a bit on the spicier side for some folks—if you want, you can rein in the spice by cutting back on the chiles. It's a treat after a meal, too, so I'll count it almost as a dessert.

2 quarts whole milk

3 dried guajillo chiles

1 (3-inch) piece of cinnamon stick

2½ cups dark semisweet chocolate chunks (I like Guittard)

½ teaspoon ground cayenne pepper

1   Combine the milk, guajillos, and cinnamon stick in a slow cooker, cover with the lid, and cook on the high setting for 2 hours.

2   Add the chocolate and cayenne to the mixture in the cooker, whisking continuously until all the chocolate has melted. Cover again and cook on the high setting for 1 hour to thicken. Whisk well before serving.

3   Best served in mugs, with biscotti for dippin'.

Red Wine–Poached Pears with Almonds & Whipped Ricotta

SLOW COOKER SIZE: **4 QUARTS**
SERVES **6**
PREP TIME: **40 MINUTES**
COOK TIME: **2 HOURS**

This is the only dessert in the book. If you want to make brownies in your slow cooker, you can Google that, but it's silly—they really steam more than bake, and you end up with a pretty one-dimensional texture. This dessert, on the other hand, uses the low-and-slow cooking to amazing results. Buy pears that are a touch on the firm side, and they will cook down to a yielding, tender bite, fully infused with the wine and aromatics.

4 cups (1⅓ bottles) good-quality red wine

1 cup sugar

3 sprigs fresh rosemary

2 bay leaves

2 star anise pods

1 strip lemon zest, plus 1 teaspoon grated lemon zest

1 strip orange zest

6 slightly unripe Anjou pears

2 cups fresh ricotta cheese

¼ cup clover honey

¼ cup whole milk

1 cup ground blanched almonds

1   Preheat a slow cooker on the high setting for at least 15 minutes.

2   In a medium saucepan, combine 2 cups of water with the wine, sugar, rosemary sprigs, bay leaves, star anise pods, and strips of lemon and orange zest. Heat to just below a boil, and then transfer the contents to the slow cooker.

3   Peel the pears. Using a melon baller or a very small spoon, carve out the cores of the pears from the bottom, keeping the pears whole. Place the peeled and cored pears in the slow cooker, stems up, cover with the lid, and cook for 2 hours on the high setting.

4   Remove the pears from the cooker and let them cool. Strain the poaching liquid into a pot and reduce the liquid over high heat until ½ cup of syrup remains, about 15 minutes.

5   Place the ricotta in a food processor fitted with the steel blade. With the processor running, drizzle in the honey and the grated lemon zest. Then thin the mixture with the milk.

6   Divide the ricotta among 6 dessert plates or shallow bowls, and nestle a poached pear in the ricotta on each plate. Shower with the almonds and drizzle with some of the reduced poaching liquid. Serve.

ACKNOWLEDGMENTS

These things don't just happen. Cookbooks are team efforts and I am blessed with an amazing array of talented people.

Chef Richard Neal is the executive chef at my original restaurant, 5&10 in Athens, but more than that, he is a friend and amazing at the craft of food, and was my culinary partner in this whole experience. Taylor Rogers is the dear soul tasked with being my assistant (i.e., brain), and he knits the patchwork of my life into some semblance of order. He put together this book in such a wonderful way. Ashley Malec is the best person ever to decipher my food language and translate it into something other people can understand. She checks and measures and calms my frenetic nature. Andrew Thomas Lee is the photographer who is tenacious yet tender, and has visionary thoughts on food. Samantha Sanford is the food stylist whose quiet demeanor and steadfast precision made the photo shoots something totally different and wonderful. All of them are responsible for this book in equal measure to me.

To Beatrice and Clementine, and their amazing mother, Mary. I can never thank you enough for being with me, watching ingredients slowly become sustenance.

To Bob Fernandez, Emily Watkins, Katrina Knight, Lynn Huba, Sarah Brendel, Claire Meneely, and Meagan Josefik. Thank you for being such a wonderful team of recipe testers.

To the team at Clarkson Potter and Penguin Random House, led by the beautiful mind of Francis Lam, my esteemed editor and dinner friend. You all the best (that needs editing).

To the fine folks at All-Clad for giving us more slow cookers than I know what to do with. Y'all make 'Merica proud. And me too.

And finally, to a world that wants to cook again, fighting back years of silly convenience, to reconnect with food in the best way possible. Cook. From scratch. Daily.

INDEX